*A special
collection
of selected
sermons
by President
Thomas S.
Monson*

THOMAS S. MONSON

Deseret Book Company
Salt Lake City, Utah

Library of Congress Catalog Card Number: 88-71770

ISBN 978-0-87579-192-0

Printed in the United States of America
Edwards Brothers, Ann Arbor, MI

10   9   8   7   6   5

CONTENTS

1

Invitation to Exaltation

2

*Tears, Trials, Trust,
Testimony*

3

Builders of Boys

4

"See Thou Tell No Man"

1

Invitation to Exaltation

Everywhere, people are in a hurry. Jet-powered planes speed their precious human cargo across broad continents and vast oceans. Appointments must be kept, tourist attractions beckon, and friends and family await the arrival of a particular flight. Modern freeways with multiple lanes carry millions of automobiles, occupied by more millions of people, in a seemingly endless stream.

Does this pulsating, mobile ribbon of humanity ever come to a halt? Is the helter-skelter pace of life at times punctuated with moments of meditation — even thoughts of timeless truths?

When compared to eternal verities, the questions of daily living are really rather trivial. What shall we have for dinner? Is there a good movie playing tonight? Have you seen the television log? Where shall we go on Saturday? These questions pale into insignificance when times of crisis arise, when loved ones are wounded, when pain enters the house of good health, or when life's candle dims and darkness threatens. Then truth and trivia are soon separated. The soul of man reaches heavenward, seeking a divine response to life's greatest questions: *Where did we come from? Why are we here? Where do we go after we leave this life?* Answers to these questions are not discovered within the covers of academia's textbooks, by dialing information, in tossing a coin, or through random selection of multiple-choice responses. These questions transcend mortality. They embrace eternity.

Where did we come from? This query is inevitably thought, if not spoken, by every parent or grandparent when a tiny infant utters its first cry. One marvels at the perfectly formed child. The tiny toes, the delicate fingers, the beautiful head, to say nothing of the hidden but marvelous circulatory, digestive, and nervous systems, all testify to the truth of a divine Creator.

The Apostle Paul told the Athenians on Mars' Hill that we are "the offspring of God." (Acts 17:29.) Since we know that our physical bodies are the offspring of our mortal parents, we must probe for the meaning of Paul's statement. The Lord has declared that "the spirit and the body are the soul of man." (D&C 88:15.) It is the spirit that is the offspring of God. The writer of Hebrews refers to Him as "the Father of spirits." (Hebrews 12:9.) The spirits of all persons are literally His "begotten sons and daughters." (D&C 76:24.)

For our contemplation of this subject we note that inspired poets have written moving messages and recorded transcendent thoughts. One writer described a newborn infant as "a sweet new blossom of humanity, fresh fallen from God's own home, to flower here on earth." (Gerald Massey.)

William Wordsworth penned this truth:

> Our birth is but a sleep and a forgetting:
> The Soul that rises with us, our life's Star,
> Hath had elsewhere its setting,
> And cometh from afar:
> Not in entire forgetfulness,

And not in utter nakedness,
But trailing clouds of glory do we come
From God, who is our home:
Heaven lies about us in our infancy!

Parents, gazing down at a tiny infant or taking the hand of a growing child, ponder their responsibility to teach, to inspire, and to provide guidance, direction, and example. While parents ponder, children, and particularly teenagers, ask the penetrating question: "Why are we here?" Usually, it is spoken silently to the soul and phrased: "Why am *I* here?"

How grateful we should be that a wise Creator fashioned an earth and placed us here, with a veil of forgetfulness on our previous existence, so that we might experience a time of testing, an opportunity to prove ourselves and qualify for all that God has prepared for us to receive.

Clearly, one primary purpose of our existence upon the earth is to obtain bodies of flesh and bones. We are here to gain experience that could come only through separation from our heavenly parents. In a thousand ways, we are privileged to choose for ourselves. Here we learn from the hard task-master of experience. We discern between good and evil. We differentiate as to the bitter and the sweet. We learn that decisions determine destiny.

While Paul taught the Philippians that individuals are called upon to "work out [their] own salvation with fear and trembling" (Philippians 2:12), the Master provided a guide we know as the Golden Rule: "All things whatsoever ye would that men should do to you, do ye even so to them." (Matthew 7:12.)

By obedience to God's commandments, we can qualify

for that "house" spoken of by Jesus when He declared: "In my Father's house are many mansions. . . . I go to prepare a place for you . . . that where I am, there ye may be also." (John 14:2-3.)

Contemplating such far-reaching matters, we reflect upon the helplessness of a newborn child. No better example can be found for total dependency. Needed is nourishment for the body and love for the soul. Mother provides both. She who, with her hand in the hand of God, descended into "the valley of the shadow of death" (Psalm 23:4) so that you and I might come forth to life, is not abandoned by God in her maternal mission.

Several years ago, the Salt Lake City newspapers published an obituary notice of a close friend, a mother and wife taken by death in the prime of her life. I visited the mortuary and joined a host of persons gathered to express condolence to the husband and motherless children. Suddenly the smallest child, Kelly, recognized me and took my hand in hers.

"Come with me," she said, and she led me to the casket in which rested the body of her beloved mother. "I'm not crying, Brother Monson, and neither must you. My mommy told me many times about death and life with Heavenly Father. I belong to my mommy and my daddy. We'll all be together again."

Through tear-moistened eyes, I recognized a beautiful and faith-filled smile. To my young friend, whose tiny hand yet clasped mine, there would never be a hopeless dawn. Sustained by her unfailing testimony, knowing that life continues beyond the grave, she, her father, her brothers, her sisters, and indeed all who share this knowledge of divine truth, can declare to the world: "Weeping may endure for a night, but joy cometh in the morning." (Psalm 30:5.)

Life moves on. Youth follows childhood, and maturity comes ever so imperceptibly. From experience we learn the need for heavenly assistance as we make our way along the pathway of mortality. We treasure the inspired thought: "God is a Father; man is a brother. Life is a mission and not a career." (President Stephen L Richards.)

God, our Father, and Jesus Christ, our Lord, have marked the way to perfection. They beckon us to follow eternal verities and to become perfect, as they are perfect. (Matthew 5:48; 3 Nephi 12:48.) The Apostle Paul likened life to a race with a clearly defined goal. To the saints at Corinth he urged: "Know ye not that they which run in a race run all, but one receiveth the prize? So run, that ye may obtain." (1 Corinthians 9:24.)

In our zeal, let us not overlook this sage counsel: "The race is not to the swift, nor the battle to the strong." (Ecclesiastes 9:11.) Actually, the prize belongs to him who endures to the end.

When I reflect on the race of life, I remember another type of race, even from childhood days. When I was about ten, my boyfriends and I would take pocketknives in hand and, from the soft wood of a willow tree, fashion small toy boats. With a triangular-shaped cotton sail in place, each would launch his crude craft in the race down the relatively turbulent waters of the Provo River. We would run along the river's bank and watch the tiny vessels sometimes bobbing violently in the swift current and at other times sailing serenely as the water deepened.

During one such race we noted that one boat led all the rest toward the appointed finish line. Suddenly the current carried it too close to a large whirlpool, and the boat heaved to its side and capsized. Around and around it was carried, unable to make its way back into the main current. At last it

5

came to an uneasy rest at the end of the pool, amid the flotsam and jetsam that surrounded it.

The toy boats of childhood had no keel for stability, no rudder to provide direction, and no source of power. Inevitably their destination was downstream — the path of least resistance.

Unlike toy boats, we have been provided divine attributes to guide our journey. We enter mortality not to float with the moving currents of life, but with the power to think, to reason, and to achieve.

We left our heavenly home and came to earth in the purity and innocence of childhood. Our Heavenly Father did not launch us on our eternal voyage without providing the means whereby we could receive from Him guidance to insure our safe return. Yes, I speak of prayer. I speak, too, of the whisperings from that still, small voice within each of us; and I do not overlook the holy scriptures, written by mariners who successfully sailed the seas we too must cross.

At some period in our mortal mission, there appears the faltering step, the wan smile, the pain of sickness — even the fading of summer, the approach of autumn, the chill of winter, and the experience we call death.

Every thoughtful person has asked himself the question best phrased by Job of old: "If a man die, shall he live again?" (Job 14:14.) Try as we may to put the question out of our thoughts, it always returns. Death comes to all mankind. It comes to the aged as they walk on faltering feet. Its summons is heard by those who have scarcely reached midway in life's journey, and often it hushes the laughter of little children.

But what of an existence beyond death? Is death the end of all? Such a question was asked of me by a young husband

and father who lay dying. I turned to the Book of Mormon and, from the book of Alma, read to him these words:

"Now, concerning the state of the soul between death and the resurrection—behold, it has been made known unto me by an angel, that the spirits of all men, as soon as they are departed from this mortal body, yea, the spirits of all men, whether they be good or evil, are taken home to that God who gave them life.

"And then shall it come to pass, that the spirits of those who are righteous are received into a state of happiness, which is called paradise, a state of rest, a state of peace, where they shall rest from all their troubles and from all care, and sorrow." (Alma 40:11-12.)

My young friend, through moist eyes and with an expression of profound gratitude, whispered a silent but eloquent "Thank you."

After the body of Jesus had lain in the tomb for three days, the spirit again entered, and the resurrected Redeemer walked forth clothed with an immortal body of flesh and bones. The answer to Job's question—"If a man die, shall he live again?"—came when Mary and others approached the tomb and saw two men in shining garments who spoke to them: "Why seek ye the living among the dead? He is not here, but is risen." (Luke 24:5-6.)

Testimonies of the resurrected Lord provide comfort and understanding.

First, from the Apostle Paul: "Christ died for our sins according to the scriptures. . . . He was buried, and . . . he rose again the third day. . . . He was seen of Cephas, then of the twelve. . . . He was seen of above five hundred brethren at once. . . . He was seen of James; then of all the apostles.

And last of all he was seen of me also, as of one born out of due time." (1 Corinthians 15:3-8.)

Second, from the combined testimony of twenty-five hundred of his other sheep, as recorded in the Book of Mormon, another testament of Jesus Christ. The resurrected Lord "spake unto them saying: Arise and come forth unto me, that ye may thrust your hands into my side, and also that ye may feel the prints of the nails in my hands and in my feet, that ye may know that I am the God of Israel, and the God of the whole earth, and have been slain for the sins of the world.

"And when they had all gone forth and had witnessed for themselves, they did cry out with one accord, saying: Hosanna! Blessed be the name of the Most High God! And they did fall down at the feet of Jesus, and did worship him." (3 Nephi 11:13-14, 16-17.)

Third, from Joseph Smith: "After the many testimonies which have been given of him, this is the testimony, last of all, which we give of him: That he lives! For we saw him, even on the right hand of God; and we heard the voice bearing record that he is the Only Begotten of the Father—that by him, and through him, and of him, the worlds are and were created, and the inhabitants thereof are begotten sons and daughters unto God." (D&C 76:22-24.)

As the result of Christ's victory over the grave, we shall all be resurrected. This is the redemption of the soul. Paul wrote: "There are . . . celestial bodies, and bodies terrestrial: but the glory of the celestial is one, and the glory of the terrestrial is another. There is one glory of the sun, and another glory of the moon, and another glory of the stars: for one star differeth from another star in glory. So also is the resurrection of the dead." (1 Corinthians 15:40-42.)

It is the celestial glory that we seek. It is in the presence of God that we desire to dwell. It is a forever family that we want membership in. Such blessings must be earned.

Where did we come from? Why are we here? Where do we go after this life? No longer need these universal questions remain unanswered. Our Heavenly Father rejoices for those who keep His commandments. He is concerned also for the lost child, the tardy teenager, the wayward youth, the delinquent parent. Tenderly the Master speaks to these, and indeed to all: "Come back. Come up. Come in. Come home. Come unto me." What eternal joy awaits when we accept His divine invitation to exaltation!

I testify that He is a teacher of truth—but He is more than a teacher. He is the exemplar of the perfect life—but He is more than an exemplar. He is the great physician—but He is more than a physician. He is the literal Savior of the world, the Son of God, the Prince of Peace, the Holy One of Israel, even the risen Lord, who declared, "I am Jesus Christ, whom the prophets testified shall come into the world. . . . I am the light and the life of the world." (3 Nephi 11:10-11.) "I am the first and the last; I am he who liveth, and I am he who was slain; I am your advocate with the Father." (D&C 110:4.)

As His witness, I testify to you that He lives!

2

Tears, Trials, Trust, Testimony

Have you ever pondered the worth of a human soul? Have you ever wondered concerning the potential that lies within each of us?

Early in my service as a member of the Council of the Twelve, I was attending a conference of the Monument Park West Stake in Salt Lake City. My companion for the conference was a member of the General Church Welfare Committee, Paul C. Child. President Child was a student of the scriptures. He had been my stake president when I was an Aaronic Priesthood youth. Now we were together as conference visitors.

When it was his opportunity to participate, President Child took the Doctrine and Covenants and left the pulpit to stand among the priesthood to whom he was directing his message. He turned to section 18 and began to read: "Remember the worth of souls is great in the sight of God. . . . And if it so be that you should labor all your days in crying repentance unto this people, and bring, save it be one soul unto me, how great shall be your joy with him in the kingdom of my Father!" (D&C 18:10, 15.)

President Child then raised his eyes from the scriptures and asked the question of the priesthood brethren: "What is

11

the worth of a human soul?" He avoided calling on a bishop, stake president, or high councilor for a response. Instead, he selected the president of an elders quorum—a brother who had been a bit drowsy and had missed the significance of the question.

The startled man responded: "Brother Child, could you please repeat the question?" The question was repeated: "What is the worth of a human soul?" I knew President Child's style. I prayed fervently for that quorum president. He remained silent for what seemed like an eternity and then declared, "Brother Child, the worth of a human soul is its capacity to become as God."

All present pondered that reply. Brother Child returned to the stand, leaned over to me, and said, "A profound reply; a profound reply!" He proceeded with his message, but I continued to reflect on that inspired response.

To reach, to teach, to touch the precious souls whom our Father has prepared for His message is a monumental task. Success is rarely simple. Generally it is preceded by tears, trials, trust, and testimony.

Think of the magnitude of the Savior's instruction to His apostles: "Go ye therefore, and teach all nations, baptizing them in the name of the Father, and of the Son, and of the Holy Ghost: teaching them to observe all things whatsoever I have commanded you: and, lo, I am with you alway, even unto the end of the world." (Matthew 28:19-20.)

The men to whom he gave this instruction were not owners of land, nor did they have the education of the learned. They were simple men—men of faith, men of devotion, men "called of God."

Paul testified to the Corinthians: "Not many wise men after the flesh, not many mighty, not many noble, are called:

But God hath chosen the foolish things of the world to confound the wise; and God hath chosen the weak things of the world to confound the things which are mighty." (1 Corinthians 1:26-27.)

On the American continent, Alma likewise counseled his son Helaman: "I say unto you, that by small and simple things are great things brought to pass." (Alma 37:6.)

Then and now, servants of God take comfort from the Master's assurance: "I am with you alway." This magnificent promise sustains brethren of the Aaronic Priesthood who are called to positions of leadership in the quorums of deacons, teachers, and priests. It encourages them in their preparations to serve in the mission field. It comforts them during those moments of discouragement which come to all. This same assurance motivates and inspires brethren of the Melchizedek Priesthood as they lead and direct the work in the wards, the stakes, and the missions. "Wherefore, be not weary in well-doing," said the Lord, "for ye are laying the foundation of a great work. And out of small things proceedeth that which is great. Behold, the Lord requireth the heart and a willing mind." (D&C 64:33-34.)

An abiding faith, a constant trust, a fervent desire have always characterized those who serve the Lord with all their hearts.

This description typified the early beginnings of missionary work following the restoration of the gospel. As early as April 1830, Phineas Young received a copy of the Book of Mormon from Samuel Smith, brother of the Prophet Joseph, and a few months later traveled to upper Canada. At Kingston, he gave the first known testimony of the restored church beyond the borders of the United States. In 1833, the Prophet Joseph Smith, Sidney Rigdon, and Freeman Nickerson traveled to Mount Pleasant, upper Canada. There they taught, they baptized, they organized a branch of the Church. At one time, in June 1835, six of the Twelve Apostles held a conference in that land.

In April 1836, Elder Heber C. Kimball and others entered the home of Parley P. Pratt and, filled with the spirit of prophecy, placed their hands on the head of Brother Pratt and declared: "Thou shalt go to Upper Canada, even to the City of Toronto, . . . and there thou shalt find a people prepared for the fulness of the gospel, and they shall receive thee, and thou shalt organize the Church among them, . . . and many shall be brought to the knowledge of the truth and shall be filled with joy; and from the things growing out of this mission, shall the fulness of the gospel spread into England, and cause a great work to be done in that land." (*Autobiography of Parley P. Pratt* [Salt Lake City: Deseret Book, 1985], p. 110.) In July 1987, the 150th anniversary of the beginning of the work in England was commemorated. We rejoice in the tremendous accomplishments of those early missionaries and those whom the Lord prepared to play such a part in the advancement of this latter-day work.

The call to serve has ever characterized the work of the Lord. It rarely comes at a convenient time. It brings humility, it provokes prayer, it inspires commitment. The call came — to Kirtland. Revelations followed. The call came — to Missouri. Persecution prevailed. The call came — to Nauvoo. Prophets died. The call came — to the Basin of the Great Salt Lake. Hardship beckoned.

That long journey, made under such difficult circumstances, was a trial of faith. But faith forged in the furnace of trials and tears is marked by trust and testimony. Only God can count the sacrifice; only God can measure the sorrow;

only God can know the hearts of those who serve Him — then and now.

Lessons from the past can quicken our memories, touch our lives, and direct our actions. We are prompted to pause and remember that divinely given promise: "Wherefore, . . . ye are on the Lord's errand; and whatsoever ye do according to the will of the Lord is the Lord's business." (D&C 64:29.)

Such a lesson was recounted on a radio and television program many remember with fondness. The program was entitled *Death Valley Days*. The narrator, known as the Old Ranger, seemed to come right into our living rooms as he would tell the tales of the West.

On one program, the Old Ranger related how the glass was obtained for the windows of the St. George Tabernacle. The glass was manufactured in the East. Then it was placed on a ship in New York that sailed forth on the long and at times perilous journey around the Cape of Good Hope and up to the west coast of America. The precious glass, stored in cartons, was then transported to San Bernardino, California, to await the overland trek to St. George.

David Cannon and the brethren in St. George had the duty to go to San Bernardino with their teams and wagons to retrieve the glass, that the tabernacle of the Lord could be completed. One problem: They needed the then astronomical sum of $800.00 to pay for the glass. They had no money. David Cannon turned to his wife and to his son and asked, "Do you think that we can raise the money, that we might obtain the glass for the tabernacle?"

His tiny son, David Jr., said, "Daddy, I know we can!" He then produced two cents of his own money and gave it to his father. Wilhelmina Cannon, David's wife, went through the secret hiding places that all women have in their houses.

15

Her search produced $3.50 in silver. The community was scoured for money, and at length the sum of $200.00 was accumulated—$600.00 short of the required amount.

David Cannon sighed the sigh of despair of one who had failed although he had tried his best. The little family was really too weary to sleep and too discouraged to eat, so they prayed. Morning dawned. The teamsters gathered with their wagons and teams, prepared to undertake the long journey to San Bernardino. But they had no $600.00. Then there came a knock at the door, and Peter Nielsen from the nearby community of Washington entered the house. He said to David Cannon, "Brother David, I have had a persistent dream that I should bring the money I had saved to expand my house — bring it to you, that you would have a purpose for it."

While all of the men gathered around the table, including little David Jr., Peter Nielsen took out a red bandanna and dropped gold pieces, one by one, upon the table. When David Cannon counted the gold pieces, they totaled $600.00 — the exact amount needed to obtain the glass. Within an hour the men waved goodbye and, with their teams, set forth on their journey to San Bernardino to retrieve the glass for the St. George tabernacle.

When that true story was told over *Death Valley Days*, David Cannon Jr. was then eighty-seven years of age. He listened to the story with rapt attention. I believe that in his mind he once again heard those gold pieces, one by one, dropping upon the table as astonished men saw with their very eyes the answer to their prayers.

Tabernacles and temples are built with more than stone and mortar, wood and glass. Particularly is this true when we speak of the temple described by the Apostle Paul: "Know ye not that ye are the temple of God, and that the Spirit of

16

God dwelleth in you?'' (1 Corinthians 3:16.) Such temples are built with faith and fasting. They are built with service and sacrifice. They are built with trials and testimonies.

If any brethren who hold the priesthood of God feel unprepared—even incapable—of responding to a call to serve, to sacrifice, to bless the lives of others, remember this truth: "Whom God calls, God qualifies." He who notes the sparrow's fall will not abandon the servant's need.

God bless those who bear the priesthood. They are "a chosen generation, a royal priesthood." (1 Peter 2:9.) May we all respond affirmatively to the Prophet Joseph, who urged: "Brethren, shall we not go on in so great a cause? Go forward and not backward. Courage, brethren; and on, on to the victory!" (D&C 128:22.)

3

Builders of Boys

In a Christmas card I received from national headquarters of Boy Scouts of America, there appeared this message: "The greatest gift a boy can have is the knowledge that a man cares enough to share a part of his life with him." I am thankful for the spirit that caring men bring to Scouting. Some have gained renown as doctors, attorneys, educators, or businessmen. Others are competent craftsmen, salesmen, engineers, or dentists. In reality, each of us is also engaged in the building trade. Our product: the building of boys.

Many of these men are skilled journeymen, even master craftsmen, with many years of service and experience in Scouting, while others are barely beginning an apprenticeship in this vital trade. All are needed. Where there is one man who is willing and able to build a boy, many more, through greed, selfishness, and lust for power, lurk in the shadows of gloom, away from the light of truth, to tear a boy down. I speak of those who peddle pornography, those who belittle morality, those who violate law, those who for filthy lucre sell a boy those products that destroy; those who put sin on a pedestal, who conceal truth, who glamorize error, who look upon a fair-haired boy as a commodity for exploitation.

The "get-rich-quick" theories, the philosophy of something for nothing, confusion of proper goals and objectives, have all combined to make our building task more difficult. The foundations of love and life-established principles are crumbling before our very eyes. They are being eroded by the forces of Lucifer. Unfortunately, some of our precious youth are even now sliding to their destruction down the slippery slopes of sin.

Throughout America, we have been screaming ever louder for more and more of the things we cannot take with us, and paying less and less attention to the real sources of the very happiness we seek. We have been measuring our fellowmen more by balance sheets and less by moral standards. We have developed frightening physical power and have fallen into pathetic spiritual weakness. We have become so concerned over the growth of our earning capacity that we have neglected the growth of our character. And our boys have been watching and learning by such an example. Perhaps this is indicative of the days in which we are living. Days of compromise and diluting of principles. Days when sin is labeled as error, when morality is relative, and when materialism emphasizes the value of expediency and the shirking of responsibility.

Well might a boy cry out in confusion in the words of Philip of old: "How can I [find my way], except some man should guide me?" (Acts 8:31.)

Our duty, our responsibility, our opportunity is to guide, to build, to inspire our boys.

> Who touches a boy by the Master's plan
> Is shaping the course of a future man,
> Is dealing with one who is human seed
> And may be a man whom the world will need.

The Master Teacher, the best Builder of all, gave us the formula: "He that findeth his life shall lose it: and he that loseth his life for my sake shall find it." (Matthew 10:39.)

May I suggest a Scouter's standard, even a performance pledge: *I will learn. I will love. I will serve.*

Are we who work with Scouts really willing to learn? Are we willing to acquire a knowledge of the programs and become familiar with the handbooks, advancement requirements, the newest and most successful suggestions and helps that the national, district, and local councils make available to us? Are we anxious and ready to discard pet theories and, while learning the program, also learn how to win the confidence and respect of our boys?

Robert W. Woodruff, American business tycoon and a friend of U. S. presidents and other great men of the world, wrote that a successful man must believe that "his joy is one of service and meaning." He offered the following "Capsule Course in Human Relations." It will also work with boys.

1. The five most important words are these: "I am proud of you."

2. The four most important words are these: "What is your opinion?"

3. The three most important words are these: "If you please."

4. The two most important words are: "Thank you."

5. The least important word is: "I."

Life is a sea upon which the proud are humbled, the shirker is exposed, and the leader is revealed. To sail it safely and reach our desired port, we need to keep our charts at hand and up to date. We need to learn by the experience of others, to stand firm for principles, to broaden our interests, and to be reliable in our discharge of duty. And through our

21

willingness to learn, education will be achieved. Henry Ford said, "An educated man is not one whose memory is trained to carry a few dates in history. He is one who can accomplish things. A man who cannot think is not an educated man, however many college degrees he may have acquired. Thinking is the hardest work anyone can do, which is probably the reason why we have so few thinkers."

When we have expressed a willingness to learn, are we ready to love? The boy assigned to the leader who really loves him will never find himself in that dreaded never-never land—never the object of concern, never the recipient of needed aid. The leader who loves his boys may never open gates of cities or doors of palaces, but his success will come as he gains entrance to the heart of a boy.

When I think of the influence of a single good man upon a boy, I think of Louis C. Jacobsen. He served the Church as a bishop and as a high councilor. He served his community as a Scouter and as a member of service clubs for boys. He was a successful industrialist, a master in the art of working with others, a father of boys. In a quiet moment he said to me, "My life changed for the better when, as the son of a poor, widowed mother, I sat dejectedly one Sunday afternoon on a dirty cement curb. I felt alone, hopeless, depressed, forsaken, rejected, and deprived. Suddenly I felt the touch of a hand upon my shoulder. I turned and looked up into the understanding face of a kind man, George Burbidge. He said, 'You're a good boy, Louis, destined for great things. May I sit down and talk with you for a moment?' "

In his neatly pressed suit, that builder of boys sat down at the level of a boy on that curb and, through love, won Louis Jacobsen's heart and changed his life. A boy had come to the crossroads of decision; a leader was there to guide him.

He stood at the crossroads all alone,
The sunlight in his face.
He had no thought for the world unknown —
He was set for a manly race.
But the roads stretched east
And the roads stretched west,
And the lad knew not which road was best,
So he chose the road that led him down,
And he lost the race and the victor's crown.
He was caught at last in an angry snare,
Because no one stood at the crossroads there
To show him the better road.

Another day at the self-same place,
A boy with high hopes stood.
He, too, was set for a manly race;
He, too, was seeking the things that were good.
But one was there who the roads did know,
And that one showed him which way to go.
So he turned from the road that would lead him
     down,
And he won the race and the victor's crown.
He walks today the highway fair,
Because one stood at the crossroads there
To show him the better way.

Once we have determined to love as well as to learn, are we ready to serve? You might ask, "How might I best serve?"

First, *serve willingly.*

Harry Emerson Fosdick wrote, "Until willingness overflows obligation, men fight as conscripts rather than following the flag as patriots. Duty is never worthily performed until it is done by one who would gladly do more if he could."

The Lord counseled, "Wherefore, be not weary in well-doing, for ye are laying the foundation of a great work. And out of small things proceedeth that which is great. Behold, the Lord requireth the heart and a willing mind; and the willing and obedient shall eat the good of the land of Zion in these last days." (D&C 64:33-34.)

Second, *serve faithfully.*

Never let it be said of us that we didn't have sufficient time. Time is precious, but life is priceless. Faithful service enables us to work as a team, which teamwork eliminates the weakness of a man standing alone and substitutes, therefore, the strength of men standing together.

Third, *serve prayerfully.*

Our task is larger than ourselves, our influence more lasting than our lives. We need the help of Almighty God. The youth we lead are created in His own image. His words thunder down through time and find lodging in our souls. "So God created man in his own image, in the image of God created he him; male and female created he them." (Genesis 1:27.) "In the image of God" was stated only of man and not any other of God's creations. Each builder of boys can be a partner with God in bringing to pass His work and His glory — the immortality and eternal life of man. (See Moses 1:39.)

Many years ago I saw a grown man cry. It wasn't his custom. The tears stemmed not from sorrow but from gratitude. My swimming coach, Charlie Welch, who perhaps helped more boys to achieve their swimming skills and successfully earn their life-saving merit badge than did any other man, was calling the roll of our swimming class at the University of Utah. His voice resounded and bounced back from the plaster walls.

The gym door opened that day in 1944 during World War

24

II, and there stood a young man in a U. S. Navy uniform. The sailor came up to Charlie and said, "Charlie, excuse me, but I want to thank you for saving my life." Charlie lifted his eyes from the roll card, put the pencil in his pocket, and asked, "What's that?" The sailor repeated, "I want to thank you for saving my life. You once told me, Charlie, that I swam like a lead ball, yet you patiently taught me to swim. Two months ago, far off in the Pacific, a Japanese torpedo sank my destroyer. As I swam my way through the murky waters and foul-tasting and ever-dangerous film of oil, I found myself saying, 'If I ever get out of this mess alive, I'm going to thank Charlie Welch for teaching me, as a Boy Scout, how to swim.' I came here today to say thank you."

Twenty athletes stood shoulder to shoulder and uttered not a word. We watched the great tears of gratitude well up in Charlie's eyes, roll down his cheeks, and tumble upon his familiar sweat shirt. Charlie Welch, a humble, prayerful, patient, and loving builder of boys, had just received his reward.

And we too, by honoring our pledge to learn, to love, to serve, can be successful in the great cause of Scouting — to build better boys today for a brighter future tomorrow.

This chapter is adapted from a talk given at the
forty-seventh annual Scouter's Convention,
February 14, 1966.

4

"See Thou Tell No Man"

Recently I approached the reception desk of a large hospital to learn the room number of a patient I had come to visit. This hospital, like almost every other in the land, was undergoing a massive expansion. Behind the desk where the receptionist sat was a magnificent plaque that bore an inscription of thanks to donors who had made possible the expansion. The name of each donor who had contributed $100,000 appeared in a flowing script, etched on an individual brass placard suspended from the main plaque by a glittering chain.

The names of the benefactors were well known. Captains of commerce, giants of industry, professors of learning—all were there. I felt gratitude for their charitable benevolence. Then my eyes rested on a brass placard that was different— it contained no name. One word, and one word only, was inscribed: "Anonymous." I smiled and wondered who the unnamed contributor could have been. Surely he or she experienced a quiet joy unknown to any other.

My thoughts turned backward in time—back to the Holy Land; back to Him who on that special mountain taught His disciples the true spirit of giving when He counseled, "Take heed that ye do not your alms before men, to be seen of them. . . . When thou doest alms, let not thy left hand know what thy right hand doeth." (Matthew 6:1, 3.)

Then, as though to indelibly impress on their souls the practical application of this sacred truth, He came down from the mountain with a great multitude following Him. "And, behold, there came a leper and worshipped him, saying, Lord, if thou wilt, thou canst make me clean. And Jesus put forth his hand, and touched him, saying, I will; be thou clean. And immediately his leprosy was cleansed. And Jesus saith unto him, See thou tell no man." (Matthew 8:2-4.)

The word anonymous had a precious meaning then. It still has.

The classics of literature, as well as the words from holy writ, teach us the endurability of anonymity. A favorite of mine is Charles Dickens's *Christmas Carol.* I can picture the trembling Ebenezer Scrooge seeing in vision the return of his former partner, Jacob Marley, though Jacob had been dead for seven years. The words of Marley penetrate my very soul, as he laments, "Not to know that any Christian spirit working kindly in its little sphere, whatever it may be, will find its mortal life too short for its vast means of usefulness. Not to know that no space of regret can make amends for one life's opportunity misused! Yet such was I. Oh! such was I!"

After a fretful night—wherein Scrooge was shown, by the Ghost of Christmas Past, the Ghost of Christmas Present, and the Ghost of Christmas Yet to Come, the true meaning of living, loving, and giving—Scrooge awakened to discover anew the freshness of life, the power of love, and the spirit of a true gift. Remembering the plight of the Bob Cratchit family, he arranged with a lad to purchase a giant turkey (the size of a boy) and sent the gift to the Cratchits. Then, with supreme joy, the reborn Ebenezer Scrooge exclaimed to himself, "He shan't know who sends it." Again the word *anonymous.*

The sands flow through the hourglass, the clock of history moves on; yet the divine truth prevails undiminished, undiluted, unchanged.

When the magnificent ocean liner *Lusitania* plunged to the bottom of the Atlantic, many lives were lost with the vessel. Unknown are many deeds of valor performed by those who perished. One man who went down with the *Lusitania* gave his life preserver to a woman, though he could not swim a stroke. It didn't really matter that he was Alfred Vanderbilt, the American multimillionaire. He did not give of worldly treasure; he gave his life. Said Emerson, "Rings and other jewels are not gifts, but apologies for gifts. The only gift is a portion of thyself."

A few years ago, a modern jetliner faltered after takeoff and plunged into the icy Potomac River. Acts of bravery and feats of heroism were in evidence that day, the most dramatic of which was one witnessed by the pilot of a rescue helicopter. The rescue rope was lowered to a struggling survivor. Rather than grasping the lifeline to safety, the man tied the line to another person, who was then lifted to safety. The rope was lowered again, and yet another was saved. Five were rescued from the icy waters. Among them was not found the anonymous hero. Unknown by name, "he left the vivid air signed with his honor." (Stephen Spender.)

It is not just in dying that one can show forth the true gift. Opportunities abound in our daily lives to demonstrate our adherence to the Master's lesson. Let me share in capsule form just three:

1. On a winter's morn, a father quietly awakened his two sons and whispered to them, "Boys, it snowed last night.

Get dressed, and we'll shovel the snow from our neighbors' walks before daylight." The party of three, dressed warmly and under cover of darkness, cleared the snow from the approaches to several homes. Father had given but one instruction to the boys: "Make no noise, and they will not know who helped them." Again, the word *anonymous*.

2. At a nursing home, two young men prepared the sacrament. While doing so, an elderly patient in a wheelchair spoke aloud the words, "I'm cold." Without a moment's hesitation, one of the young men walked over to her, removed his own jacket, placed it about the patient's shoulders, gave her a loving pat on the arm, and then returned to the sacrament table. The sacred emblems were then blessed and passed to the assembled patients.

Following the meeting, I said to the young man, "What you did here today I shall long remember."

He replied, "I worried that without my jacket I would not be properly dressed to bless the sacrament."

I responded, "Never was one more properly dressed for such an occasion than were you."

I know not his name. He remains anonymous.

3. In far-off Europe, beyond a curtain of iron and a wall called Berlin, I visited, with a handful of Latter-day Saints, a small cemetery. It was a dark night, and a cold rain had been falling throughout the entire day. We had come to visit the grave of a missionary who many years before had died while in the service of the Lord. A hushed silence shrouded the scene as we gathered about the grave. With a flashlight illuminating the headstone, I read the inscription:

> Joseph A. Ott
> Born: 12 December 1870 — Virgin, Utah
> Died: 10 January 1896 — Dresden, Germany

Then the light revealed that this grave was unlike any other in the cemetery. The marble headstone had been polished, weeds such as those which covered other graves had been carefully removed, and in their place was an immaculately edged bit of lawn and some beautiful flowers that told of tender and loving care. I asked, "Who has made this grave so attractive?" My query was met by silence.

At last a twelve-year-old deacon acknowledged that he had wanted to render this unheralded kindness and, without prompting from parents or leaders, had done so. He said that he just wanted to do something for a missionary who had given his life while in the service of the Lord. I thanked him, and then I asked all there to safeguard his secret, that his gift might remain anonymous.

Perhaps no one in my reading has portrayed this teaching of the Master quite so memorably or so beautifully as Henry Van Dyke in his never-to-be-forgotten "The Mansion." In this classic story is featured one John Weightman, a man of means, a dispenser of political power, a successful citizen. His philosophy toward giving can be gained from his own statement: "Of course you have to be careful how you give, in order to secure the best results — no indiscriminate giving — no pennies in beggars' hats! . . . Try to put your gifts where they can be identified and do good all around."

One evening John Weightman sat in his comfortable chair at his library table and perused the papers spread before him. There were descriptions and pictures of the Weightman wing of the hospital and the Weightman Chair of Political Jurisprudence, as well as an account of the opening of the Weightman Grammar School. John Weightman felt satisfied.

Then he picked up the family Bible, which lay on the table, turned to a passage, and read these words: "Lay not

31

up for yourselves treasures upon earth, where moth and rust doth corrupt, and where thieves break through and steal: But lay up for yourselves treasures in heaven." (Matthew 6:19-20.)

The book seemed to float away from him. He leaned forward upon the table, his head resting on his folded hands. He slipped into a deep sleep.

In his dream, John Weightman was transported to the Heavenly City. A guide met him and others whom he had known in life and said that he would conduct them to their heavenly homes.

The group paused before a beautiful mansion and heard the guide say, "This is the home for you, Dr. McLean. Go in; there is no more sickness here, no more death, nor sorrow, nor pain; for your old enemies are all conquered. But all the good that you have done for others, all the help that you have given, all the comfort that you have brought, all the strength and love that you bestowed upon the suffering, are here; for we have built them all into this mansion for you."

A devoted husband of an invalid wife was shown a lovely mansion, as were a mother, early widowed, who had reared an outstanding family, and a paralyzed young woman who had lain for thirty years upon her bed — helpless but not hopeless — succeeding by a miracle of courage in her single aim: never to complain, but always to impart a bit of her joy and peace to everyone who came near her.

By this time, John Weightman was impatient to see what mansion awaited him. As he and the Keeper of the Gate walked on, the homes became smaller — then smaller. At last they stood in the middle of a dreary field and beheld a hut, hardly big enough for a shepherd's shelter. Said the guide, "This is your mansion, John Weightman."

In desperation, John Weightman argued, "Have you not heard that I have built a schoolhouse; a wing of a hospital; . . . three . . . churches?"

"Wait," the guide cautioned. "They were not ill done. But they were all marked and used as foundations for the name and mansion of John Weightman in the world. . . . Verily, you have had your reward for them. Would you be paid twice?"

A sadder but wiser John Weightman spoke more slowly: "What is it that counts here?"

Came the reply, "Only that which is truly given. Only that good which is done for the love of doing it. Only those plans in which the welfare of others is the master thought. Only those labors in which the sacrifice is greater than the reward. Only those gifts in which the giver forgets himself."

John Weightman was awakened by the sound of the clock chiming the hour of seven. He had slept the night through. As it turned out, he yet had a life to live, love to share, and gifts to give.

May this truth guide our lives. May we look upward as we press forward in the service of our God and our fellowmen. And may we incline an ear toward Galilee, that we might hear perhaps an echo of the Savior's teachings: "Do not your alms before men, to be seen of them." "Let not thy left hand know what thy right hand doeth." And of our good deeds: "See thou tell no man." (Matthew 6:1, 3; 8:4.) Our hearts will then be lighter, our lives brighter, and our souls richer.

Loving service anonymously given may be unknown to man—but the gift and the giver are known to God.

5

Your Liahona of Light

Have you ever cleaned an attic or rummaged through an old storeroom? One discovers a bit of history and a whole lot of sentiment. A few weeks ago we emptied the attic of our mountain cabin. Seventy years of treasures, each with its own special memory, passed in review. Leading the parade was an old high chair with metal wheels. This was followed by glass milk bottles that once had pasteboard caps, and a copy of *Life Magazine* with a story from World War II.

Featured in the magazine was an account of a once proud airplane, a mighty bomber, found rather well preserved in an isolated corner of the vast Sahara Desert. The bomber and crew had participated in the famous raid over Romania's Ploiesti oil fields. The craft had been struck by anti-aircraft fire, which completely destroyed its communication and navigational equipment. As the stricken plane turned toward its desert landing field, a sudden sand storm obliterated familiar points of reference. The field's landing lights were shrouded by sand. The plane droned on, even far beyond the landing field, into the desert wastes until, with fuel exhausted, it settled on the Sahara, never to fly again. All crew members perished. Home and the safety and shelter there to be found had been denied. Victory, hopes, dreams — all had been swallowed by the silence of the desert's dust.

Centuries earlier, a righteous and loving father by the name of Lehi took his beloved family into a desert wasteland. He journeyed in response to the voice of the Lord. But the Lord did not decree that such a "flight" be undertaken without Divine help. The words of Nephi describe the gift provided on the morning of the historic trek: "And it came to pass that as my father arose in the morning, and went forth to the tent door, to his great astonishment he beheld upon the ground a round ball of curious workmanship; and it was of fine brass. And within the ball were two spindles; and the one pointed the way whither we should go into the wilderness." (1 Nephi 16:10.)

War and manmade means of destruction could not confuse or destroy this curious compass. Neither could the sudden desert sandstorms render useless its guiding powers. The prophet Alma explained that this "Liahona," as it was called, was a compass prepared by the Lord. It worked for Lehi and his followers according to their faith and pointed the way they should go. (See Alma 37:38-40.)

The same Lord who provided a Liahona for Lehi provides for you and for me today a rare and valuable gift to give direction to our lives, to mark the hazards to our safety, and to chart the way, even safe passage — not to a promised land, but to our heavenly home. The gift to which I refer is known as a patriarchal blessing. Every worthy member of the Church is entitled to receive such a precious and priceless personal treasure.

"Patriarchal blessings," wrote the First Presidency in a letter to stake presidents in 1958, "contemplate an inspired declaration of the lineage of the recipient and, when so moved upon by the Spirit, an inspired and prophetic statement of the life mission of the recipient, together with such blessings, cautions, and admonitions as the patriarch may be prompted to give for the accomplishment of such life's mission, it being always made clear that the realization of all promised blessings is conditioned upon faithfulness to the gospel of our Lord, whose servant the patriarch is."

Who is this man, this patriarch, through whom such seership and priesthood power flow? How is he called? The Council of the Twelve Apostles has special responsibility pertaining to the calling of such a man. From my own experience, I testify that patriarchs are called of God by prophecy. How else could our Heavenly Father reveal those to whom such prophetic powers are to be given? A patriarch holds an ordained office in the Melchizedek Priesthood. The patriarchal office, however, is one of blessing, not of administration. I have never called a man to this sacred office but what I have felt the Lord's guiding influence in the decision. May I share with you one treasured experience.

Many years ago I was assigned to name a patriarch for a stake in Logan, Utah. I found such a man, wrote his name on a slip of paper, and placed the note inside my scriptures. My further review revealed that another worthy patriarch had moved to this same area, making unnecessary the naming of a new patriarch. None was named.

Nine years later I was again assigned a stake conference in Logan. Once more a patriarch was needed for the stake I was to visit. I had been using a new set of scriptures for several years and had them in my briefcase. However, as I prepared to leave my home for the drive to Logan, I took from the bookcase shelf an older set of scriptures, leaving the new ones at home. During the conference I began my search for a patriarch: a worthy man, a blameless servant of God, one filled with faith, characterized by kindness. Pondering these requirements, I opened my scriptures and discovered the slip of paper placed there long years before. I read the name written on the paper: Cecil B. Kenner. I asked the stake presidency if by chance Brother Kenner lived in this particular stake. He did. Cecil B. Kenner was that day ordained a patriarch.

Patriarchs are humble men. They are students of the scriptures. They stand before God as the means whereby the blessings of heaven can flow from that eternal source to the recipient on whose head rests the hands of the patriarch. The patriarch may not be a man of letters, a possessor of worldly wealth, or a holder of distinguished office. He must, however, be blessed with priesthood power and personal purity. To reach to heaven for divine guidance and inspiration, a patriarch is to be a man of love, a man of compassion, a man of judgment, a man of God.

A patriarchal blessing is a revelation to the recipient, even a white line down the middle of the road, to protect, inspire, and motivate activity and righteousness. A patriarchal blessing literally contains chapters from the recipient's book of eternal possibilities. I say eternal, for just as life is eternal, so is a patriarchal blessing. What may not come to fulfillment in this life may occur in the next. We do not govern God's timetable. "For my thoughts are not your thoughts, neither are your ways my ways, saith the Lord. For as the heavens are higher than the earth, so are my ways higher than your ways, and my thoughts than your thoughts." (Isaiah 55:8-9.)

Your patriarchal blessing is yours and yours alone. It may be brief or lengthy, simple or profound. Length and language do not a patriarchal blessing make. It is the spirit that conveys the true meaning. Your blessing is not to be folded neatly and tucked away. It is not to be framed or published. Rather, it is to be read. It is to be loved. It is to be followed.

Your patriarchal blessing will see you through the darkest night. It will guide you through life's dangers. Unlike the struggling bomber of yesteryear, lost in the desert wastes, the sands and storms of life will not destroy you on your eternal flight. Your patriarchal blessing is to you a personal Liahona to chart your course and guide your way.

In Lewis Carroll's classic *Alice's Adventures in Wonderland,* Alice finds herself coming to a crossroads with two paths before her, each stretching onward but in opposite directions. She is confronted by the Cheshire Cat, of whom she asks, "Which path shall I take?"

The cat answers, "That depends where you want to go. If you do not know where you want to go, it doesn't really matter which path you take."

Unlike Alice, each of us knows where he or she wants to go. It does matter which way we go, for the path we follow in this life leads to the path we shall follow in the next.

Patience may be required as we watch, wait, and work for a promised blessing to be fulfilled.

One afternoon Percy K. Fetzer, a righteous patriarch, came to my office by appointment. He was weeping as we visited together. He explained that he had just returned from the land of Poland, where he had been privileged to give patriarchal blessings to our worthy members there. After a long pause, the patriarch revealed that he had been impressed to promise to members of a German-speaking family by the name of Konietz declarations that could not be fulfilled. He had promised missions. He had promised temple blessings. These were beyond the reach of those whom he had blessed.

He whispered how he had tried to withhold the promises he knew were unattainable. It had been no use. The inspiration had come, the promises had been spoken, the blessings had been provided.

"What shall I do? What can I say?" he repeated to me.

I replied, "Brother Fetzer, these blessings have not come from you; they have been given of God. Let us kneel and pray to Him for their fulfillment."

Within several years of that prayer, an unanticipated pact was signed between the Federal Republic of Germany and the Polish nation, which provided that German nationals trapped in Poland at war's end could now enter Germany. The Konietz family, whose members had received these special patriarchal blessings, went to live in West Germany. I had the privilege of ordaining the father a bishop in the Dortmund Stake of the Church. The family then made that long-awaited trek to the temple in Switzerland. They dressed in clothing of spotless white. They knelt at a sacred altar to await that ordinance which binds father, mother, brothers, and sisters not only for time, but for all eternity. He who pronounced that sacred sealing ceremony was the temple president. More than this, however, he was the same servant of the Lord, Percy K. Fetzer, who as a patriarch years before had provided those precious promises in the patriarchal blessings he had bestowed.

Your patriarchal blessing is your passport to peace in this life. It is a Liahona of light to guide you unerringly to your heavenly home.

6

The Long Line of the Lonely

The Epistle of James has long been a favorite book of the Holy Bible. I find James's brief message both heart-warming and filled with life. Each of us can quote that well-known passage, "If any of you lack wisdom, let him ask of God, that giveth to all men liberally, and upbraideth not; and it shall be given him." (James 1:5.) How many of us, however, remember James's definition of religion: "Pure religion and undefiled before God and the Father is this, To visit the fatherless and widows in their affliction, and to keep himself unspotted from the world." (James 1:27.)

The word *widow* appears to have had a most significant meaning to our Lord. He cautioned His disciples to beware the example of the scribes, who feigned righteousness by their long apparel and their lengthy prayers, but who devoured the houses of widows. (See Mark 12:38, 40.)

To the Nephites came this warning: "I will come near to you in judgment; and I will be a swift witness against . . . those that oppress the . . . widow." (3 Nephi 24:5.)

To the Prophet Joseph Smith He directed, "The storehouse shall be kept by the consecrations of the church; and widows and orphans shall be provided for, as also the poor." (D&C 83:6.)

Such teachings were not new then. They are not new now. Consistently the Master has taught, by example, His concern for the widow. To the grieving widow at Nain, bereft of her only son, He came personally; and to the dead son He restored the breath of life — and to the astonished widow her son. To the widow at Zarephath, who with her son faced imminent starvation, He sent the prophet Elijah with the power to teach faith as well as provide food.

We may say to ourselves, "But that was long ago and ever so far away." I respond, "Is there a city called Zarephath near your home? Is there a town known as Nain?" We may know our cities as Columbus or Coalville, Detroit or Denver. Whatever the name, there lives within each city the widow deprived of her companion and often her child. The need is the same. The affliction is real.

The widow's home is generally not large or ornate. Frequently it is modest in size and humble in appearance. Often it is tucked away at the top of the stairs or the back of the hallway and consists of but one room. To such homes He sends you and me.

There may exist an actual need for food, clothing — even shelter. Such can be supplied. Almost always there remains the hope for that special hyacinth to feed the soul.

> Go visit the lonely, the dreary;
> Go comfort the weeping, the weary;
> Go scatter kind deeds on your way.
> Oh, make the world brighter today!
> —Mrs. Frank A. Breck

The ranks of those in special need grow larger day by day. Note the obituary page of your newspaper. Here the drama of life unfolds to view. Death comes to all mankind.

42

It comes to the aged as they walk on faltering feet. Its summons is heard by those who have scarcely reached midway in life's journey, and it often hushes the laughter of little children.

After the funeral flowers fade, the well wishes of friends become memories, and the prayers offered and the words spoken dim in the corridors of the mind, those who grieve frequently join that vast throng I shall entitle "The Long Line of the Lonely." Missed are the laughter of children, the commotion of teenagers, and the tender, loving concern of a departed companion. The clock ticks more loudly, time passes more slowly, and four walls do indeed a prison make.

Hopefully, all of us may again hear the echo of words spoken by the Master: "Inasmuch as ye have done it unto one of the least of these . . . ye have done it unto me." (Matthew 25:40.)

As we resolve to minister more diligently to those in need, let us remember to include our children in these learning lessons of life.

I have many memories of my boyhood. Anticipating Sunday dinner was one of them. Just as we children hovered at our so-called starvation level and sat anxiously at the table with the aroma of roast beef filling the room, Mother would say to me, "Tommy, before we eat, take this plate I've prepared down the street to Old Bob and hurry back." I could never understand why we couldn't first eat and later deliver his plate of food. I never questioned aloud but would run down to Bob's house and then wait anxiously as his aged feet brought him eventually to the door. Then I would hand him the plate of food. He would present to me the clean plate from the previous Sunday and offer me a dime as pay for my services. My answer was always the same: "I can't accept the money. My mother would tan my hide." He would then run his wrinkled hand through my blond hair and say, "My boy, you have a wonderful mother. Tell her thank you." You know, I think I never did tell her. I sort of felt Mother didn't need to be told. She seemed to sense his gratitude. I remember, too, that Sunday dinner always seemed to taste a bit better after I had returned from my errand.

Old Bob came into our lives in an interesting way. He was a widower in his eighties when the house in which he was living was to be demolished. I heard him tell my grandfather his plight as the three of us sat on the old front-porch swing. With a plaintive voice, he said to Grandfather, "Mr. Condie, I don't know what to do. I have no family. I have no place to go. I have no money."

I wondered how Grandfather would answer. Slowly he reached into his pocket and took from it that old leather purse from which, in response to my hounding, he had produced many a penny or nickel for a special treat. This time he removed a key and handed it to Old Bob. Tenderly he said, "Bob, here is the key to that house I own next door. Take it. Move in your things. Stay as long as you like. There will be no rent to pay and nobody will ever put you out again."

Tears welled up in the eyes of Old Bob, coursed down his cheeks, then disappeared in his long, white beard. Grandfather's eyes were also moist. I spoke no word, but that day my grandfather stood ten feet tall. I was proud to bear his given name. Though I was but a boy, that lesson has influenced my life.

Each of us has his own way of remembering. At Christmastime I take delight in visiting the widows and widowers from the ward where I served as bishop. There were eighty-seven then, just nine today. On such visits, I never know what to expect, but this I do know: visits like these provide for me the Christmas spirit, which is, in reality, the Spirit of Christ.

Come with me, and we'll together make a call or two.

At a nursing home on First South, we might interrupt, as I did a few years ago, a professional football game. There, before the TV, were seated two widows. They were warmly and beautifully dressed — and absorbed in the game. I asked, "Who's winning?" They responded, "We don't even know who's playing, but at least it's company." I sat between those two angels and explained the game of football. I enjoyed the best contest I can remember. I may have missed a meeting, but I harvested a memory.

Let's hurry along to Redwood Road. There is a much larger home here where many widows reside. Most are seated in the well-lighted living room. But in her bedroom, alone, is one on whom I must call. She hasn't spoken a word since a devastating stroke some years ago. But then, who knows what she hears, so I speak of good times together. There isn't a flicker of recognition, not a word spoken. In fact, an attendant asks if I am aware that this patient hasn't uttered a word for years. It makes no difference. Not only have I enjoyed my one-sided conversation with her — I have communed with God.

There's another nursing home on West Temple, where four widows reside. You never walk up the pathway but what you notice the parted curtain, as one inside waits hour after hour for the approaching step of a friend. What a welcome! Good times are remembered, perhaps a gift given, a blessing provided; but then it is time to leave. Never could I depart without first responding to the request of a widow almost one hundred years of age. Though she was blind, she would say, "Bishop, you're to speak at my funeral and recite from memory Alfred Lord Tennyson's poem 'Crossing the Bar.' Let's hear you do it right now!" I would proceed:

Sunset and evening star,
    And one clear call for me,
And may there be no moaning of the bar,
    When I put out to sea.

Twilight and evening bell,
    And after that the dark!
And may there be no sadness of farewell
    When I embark;

For tho' from out our bourne of time and place
    The flood may bear me far,
I hope to see my Pilot face to face
    When I have crossed the bar.

Tears came easily, and then, with a smile, she would say, "Tommy, that was pretty good, but see that you do it a wee bit better at the funeral." I later honored her request.

When our beloved President Spencer W. Kimball met once with some visitors from a country where want is present, he did not ask regarding statistics, but rather inquired, "Do our people have enough to eat? Are the widows cared for?" He was concerned.

During the administration of President George Albert Smith, there lived in our ward an impoverished widow who cared for her three mature daughters, each of whom was an invalid. They were large in size and almost totally helpless. To this dear woman fell the task of bathing, feeding, dressing, and caring for her girls. Means were limited. Outside help was nonexistent. Then came the blow that the house she rented was to be sold. What was she to do? Where would she go? The bishop went to the Church Office Building to inquire if there were some way the house could be purchased. It was so small, the price so reasonable. The request was considered, then denied. A heartsick bishop was leaving the front door of the building when he met President George Albert Smith. After the exchange of greetings, President Smith inquired, "What brings you to the headquarters building?" He listened carefully as the bishop explained, but said nothing. He then excused himself for a few minutes. He returned wearing a smile and directed, "Go upstairs to the fourth floor. A check is waiting there for you. Buy the house."

"But the request was denied."

Again President Smith smiled and said, "It has just been reconsidered and approved." The home was purchased. That dear widow lived there and cared for her daughters until each of them had passed away. Then she, too, went home to God and to her heavenly reward.

The leadership of the Church is mindful of the widow, the widower, the lonely. Can we be less concerned? We remember that during the meridian of time a bright, particular star shone in the heavens. Wise men followed it and found the Christ child. Today wise men still look heavenward and again see a bright, particular star. It will guide you and me to our opportunities. The burden of the downtrodden will be lifted, the cry of the hungry will be stilled, the lonely heart will be comforted—and souls will be saved. Yours, theirs, and mine. If we truly listen, we may hear that voice from far away say to us, as it spoke to another, "Well done, thou good and faithful servant." (Matthew 25:21.)

7

Christmas Gifts, Christmas Blessings

What did you get for Christmas?" This is the universal question among children for days following that most celebrated holiday of the year. A small girl might reply, "I received a doll, a new dress, and a fun game." A boy might respond, "I received a pocketknife, a train, and a truck with lights." Newly acquired possessions are displayed and admired as Christmas day dawns, then departs.

The gifts so acquired are fleeting. Dolls break, dresses wear out, and fun games become boring. Pocketknives are lost, trains do nothing but go in circles, and trucks are abandoned when the batteries that power them dim and die.

If we change but one word in our Christmas question, the outcome is vastly different. "What did you *give* for Christmas?" prompts stimulating thought and causes tender feelings to well up and memory's fires to glow ever brighter.

Giving, not getting, brings to full bloom the Christmas spirit. Enemies are forgiven, friends remembered, and God obeyed. The spirit of Christmas illuminates the picture window of the soul, and we look out upon the world's busy life and become more interested in people than things. To catch the real meaning of the spirit of Christmas, we need only drop the last syllable and it becomes the spirit of Christ.

> What can I give Him,
> Poor as I am?
> If I were a shepherd
> I would bring a lamb.
> If I were a Wise Man
> I would do my part,
> Yet what can I give Him?
> Give my heart.
> —Christina Georgina Rosetti

One ever remembers that Christmas day when giving replaced getting. In my life, this took place in my tenth year. As Christmas approached, I yearned as only a boy can yearn for an electric train. My desire was not to receive the economical and everywhere-to-be-found windup model train; rather, I wanted one that operated through the miracle of electricity. The times were those of economic depression; yet Mother and Dad, through some sacrifice I am sure, presented to me on Christmas morning a beautiful electric train.

For hours I operated the transformer, watching the engine first pull its cars forward, then push them backward around the track. Mother entered the living room and said to me that she had purchased a windup train for Mrs. Hansen's son, Mark, who lived down the lane. I asked if I could see the train. The engine was short and blocky, not long and sleek like the expensive model I had received. However, I did take notice of an oil tanker car that was part of his inexpensive set. My train had no such car, and pangs of envy began to be felt. I put up such a fuss that Mother succumbed to my pleadings and handed me the oil tanker car. She said,

"If you need it more than Mark, you take it." I put it with my train set and felt pleased with the result.

Mother and I took the remaining cars and the engine down to Mark Hansen. The young boy was a year or two older than I. He had never anticipated such a gift and was thrilled beyond words. He wound the key in his engine, it not being electric like mine, and was overjoyed as the engine and two cars, plus a caboose, went around the track.

Then Mother wisely asked, "What do you think of Mark's train, Tommy?"

I felt a keen sense of guilt and became very much aware of my selfishness. I said to Mother, "Wait just a moment. I'll be right back."

As swiftly as my legs could carry me, I ran home, picked up the oil tanker car plus an additional car from my train set, and ran back down the lane to the Hansen home, joyfully saying to Mark, "We forgot to bring two cars that belong to your train." Mark coupled the two extra cars to his set. I watched the engine make its labored way around the track and felt supreme joy, difficult to describe and impossible to forget. The spirit of Christmas had filled my very soul.

That experience made it somewhat easier for me to make a difficult decision just one year later. Again Christmastime had come. We were preparing for the oven a gigantic turkey and anticipating the savory feast that awaited. A neighborhood pal of mine asked a startling question: "What does turkey taste like?"

I responded, "Oh, about like chicken tastes."

Again a question: "What does chicken taste like?"

It was then that I realized my friend had never eaten chicken or turkey. I asked what his family was going to have for Christmas dinner. There was no prompt response, just a downcast glance and the comment, "I dunno. There's nothing in the house."

I pondered a solution. There was none. I had no turkeys, no chickens, no money. Then I remembered I did have two pet rabbits. Immediately I took them to my friend and handed the box to him with the comment, "Here, take these two rabbits. They're good to eat—just like chicken."

He took the box, climbed the fence, and headed for home—a Christmas dinner safely assured. Tears came easily to me as I closed the door to the empty rabbit hutch. But I was not sad. A warmth, a feeling of indescribable joy, filled my heart. It was a memorable Christmas.

In New York City, there presides in a stake of the Church a young man who, as a boy of thirteen, led his quorum of deacons in a successful search for the Christmas spirit. He and his companions lived in a neighborhood in which many elderly widows of limited means resided. All the year long, the boys had saved and planned for a glorious Christmas party. They were thinking of themselves, until the Christmas spirit prompted them to think of others. Frank, as their leader, suggested to his companions that the funds they had saved so carefully be used not for the planned party, but rather for the benefit of three elderly widows who resided together.

The boys made their plans. As their bishop, I needed but to follow. With the enthusiasm of a new adventure, the boys purchased a giant roasting chicken, the potatoes, the vegetables, the cranberries, and all that comprises the traditional Christmas feast. To the widows' home they went, carrying their gifts of treasure. Through the snow and up the path to the tumbledown porch they came. A knock at the door, the sound of slow footsteps, and then they met.

In the unmelodic voices characteristic of thirteen-year-olds, the boys sang: "Silent night, holy night; all is calm, all is bright." They then presented their gifts. Angels on that glorious night of long ago sang no more beautifully, nor did Wise Men present gifts of greater meaning. I gazed at the faces of those wonderful women and thought to myself, "Somebody's mother." I then looked on the countenances of those noble boys and reflected, "Somebody's son." There then passed through my mind the words of the immortal poem by Mary Dow Brine:

> The woman was old and ragged and gray
> And bent with the chill of the Winter's day.
> The street was wet with a recent snow,
> And the woman's feet were aged and slow.
> She stood at the crossing and waited long,
> Alone, uncared for, amid the throng
> Of human beings who passed her by,
> Nor heeded the glance of her anxious eye.
>
> Down the street, with laughter and shout,
> Glad in the freedom of "school let out,"
> Came the boys like a flock of sheep,
> Hailing the snow piled white and deep. . . .
>
> [One] paused beside her and whispered low,
> "I'll help you cross, if you wish to go." . . .
>
> "She's somebody's mother, boys, you know,
> For all she's aged and poor and slow.
> And I hope some fellow will lend a hand
> To help my mother, you understand,
> If ever she's poor and old and gray,
> When her own dear boy is far away."
> And "somebody's mother" bowed low her head

In her home that night, and the prayer she said
Was, "God be kind to the noble boy,
Who is somebody's son, and pride and joy!"

Not one of those boys ever forgot that precious pilgrimage. Christmas gifts had become Christmas blessings.

Times change, years speed by; but Christmas continues sacred. It is through giving, rather than getting, that the spirit of Christ enters our lives. God still speaks. He prompts. He guides. He blesses. He gives.

Many years ago, President Harold B. Lee recounted to me an experience of a President Ballantyne who grew up in Star Valley, Wyoming. This is harsh country. The summers are short and fleeting, while the winters linger and chill. President Ballantyne told of a special Christmas season from his boyhood days. He said:

"Father had a large family; and sometimes after we had our harvest, there was not much left after expenses were paid. So Father would have to go away and hire out to some of the big ranchers for maybe a dollar a day. He earned little more than enough to take care of himself, with very little to send home to Mother and the children. Things began to get pretty skimpy for us.

"We had our family prayers around the table; and it was on one such night when Father was gone that we gathered and Mother poured out of a pitcher, into the glass of each one, milk divided among the children—but none for herself. And I, sensing that the milk in the pitcher was all that we had, pushed mine over to Mother and said, 'Here, Mother. You drink mine.'

" 'No. Mother is not hungry tonight.'

"It worried me. We drank our milk and went to bed, but

I could not sleep. I got up and tiptoed down the stairs, and there was Mother, in the middle of the floor, kneeling in prayer. She did not hear me as I came down in my bare feet, and I dropped to my knees and heard her say, 'Heavenly Father, there is no food in our house. Please, Father, touch the heart of somebody so that my children will not be hungry in the morning.'

"When she finished her prayer, she looked around and saw that I had heard; and she said to me, somewhat embarrassed, 'Now, you run along, son. Everything will be all right.'

"I went to bed, assured by Mother's faith. The next morning, I was awakened by the sounds of pots and pans in the kitchen and the aroma of cooking food. I went down to the kitchen, and I said, 'Mother, I thought you said there was no food.'

"All she said to me was, 'Well, my boy, didn't you think the Lord would answer my prayer?' I received no further explanation than that.

"Years passed, and I went away to college. I got married, and I returned to see the old folks. Bishop Gardner, now reaching up to a ripe age, said to me, 'My son, let me tell you of a Christmas experience that I had with your family. I had finished my chores, and we had had supper. I was sitting by the fireplace reading the newspaper. Suddenly, I heard a voice that said, "Sister Ballantyne doesn't have any food in her house." I thought it was my wife speaking and said, "What did you say, Mother?" She came in wiping her hands on her apron and said, "Did you call me, Father?"

" ' "No, I didn't say anything to you, but I heard a voice which spoke to me."

" ' "What did it say?" she asked.

55

" ' "It said that Sister Ballantyne didn't have any food in her house."

" ' "Well, then," said Mother, "you had better put on your shoes and your coat and take some food to Sister Ballantyne." In the dark of that winter's night, I harnessed the team and placed in the wagon bed a sack of flour, a quarter section of beef, some bottled fruit, and loaves of newly baked bread. The weather was cold, but a warm glow filled my soul as your mother welcomed me and I presented her with the food. God had heard a mother's prayer.' "

Heavenly Father is ever mindful of those who need, who seek, who trust, who pray, and who listen when He speaks. "For God so loved the world, that he gave his only begotten Son, that whosoever believeth in him should not perish, but have everlasting life." (John 3:16.) God's gift becomes our blessing. May every heart open wide and welcome Him—Christmas day and always.

8

The Spirit Giveth Life

Recently I visited the Missionary Training Center at Provo, Utah, where missionaries who have been called to serve throughout the world are devotedly learning the fundamentals of the languages spoken by the people whom they shall teach and to whom they shall testify.

Vaguely familiar to me were the conversations in Spanish, French, German, and Swedish. Totally foreign to me, and perhaps to most of the missionaries, were the sounds of Japanese, Chinese, and Finnish. One marvels at the devotion and total concentration of these young men and women as they grapple with the unfamiliar and learn the difficult.

I am told that on occasion when a missionary in training feels that the Spanish he is called upon to master appears overwhelming or just too hard to learn, he is placed during the luncheon break next to missionaries studying the complex languages of the Orient. He listens. Suddenly Spanish becomes not too overpowering, and he eagerly returns to his study.

There is one language, however, that is common to each missionary — the language of the Spirit. It is not learned from textbooks written by men of letters, nor is it acquired through reading and memorization. The language of the Spirit comes to him who seeks with all his heart to know God and keep His divine commandments. Proficiency in this language permits one to breach barriers, overcome obstacles, and touch the human heart.

In his second epistle to the Corinthians, Paul the apostle urges that we turn from the narrow confinement of the letter of the law and seek the open vista of opportunity that the Spirit provides. I love and cherish his statement: "The letter killeth, but the spirit giveth life." (2 Corinthians 3:6.)

In a day of danger or a time of trial, such knowledge, such hope, such understanding bring comfort to the troubled mind and grieving heart. The entire message of the New Testament breathes a spirit of awakening to the human soul. Shadows of despair are dispelled by rays of hope, sorrow yields to joy, and the feeling of being lost in the crowd of life vanishes with the certain knowledge that our Heavenly Father is mindful of each of us.

The Savior provided assurance of this truth when He taught that not even a sparrow shall fall to the ground unnoticed by our Father. He then concluded the beautiful thought by saying, "Fear ye not therefore; ye are of more value than many sparrows. Whosoever therefore shall confess me before men, him will I confess also before my Father which is in heaven." (Matthew 10:29-32.)

We live in a complex world with daily challenges. There is a tendency to feel detached, even isolated, from the Giver of every good gift. We worry that we walk alone.

From the bed of pain, from the pillow wet with the tears of loneliness, we are lifted heavenward by that divine assurance and precious promise, "I will not fail thee, nor forsake thee." (Joshua 1:5.)

Such comfort is priceless as we journey along the pathway of mortality, with its many forks and turnings. Rarely is the assurance communicated by a flashing sign or a loud voice. Rather, the language of the Spirit is gentle, quiet, uplifting to the heart and soothing to the soul.

At times, the answers to our questions and the responses to our daily prayers come to us through silent promptings of the Spirit. As William Cowper wrote:

> God moves in a mysterious way
> His wonders to perform;
> He plants His footsteps in the sea
> And rides upon the storm.
>
> Judge not the Lord by feeble sense,
> But trust Him for His grace;
> Behind a frowning Providence
> He hides a smiling face.

We watch. We wait. We listen for that still, small voice. When it speaks, wise men and women obey. Promptings of the Spirit are not to be postponed.

To address such a sacred subject, may I refer not to the writings of others, but to the actual experiences of my life. I testify to their truth, for I lived them. I share with you three cherished examples of what President David O. McKay identified as "heart petals" — the language of the Spirit, the promptings from a heavenly source.

First, the inspiration that attends a call to serve.

Every bishop can testify to the promptings that attend calls to serve in the Church. Frequently the call seems to be for the benefit not so much of those to be taught or led as for the person who is to teach or lead.

As a bishop, I worried about any members who were inactive, not attending, not serving. Such was my thought as I drove down the street where Ben and Emily lived. They were older, in the twilight period of life. Aches and pains of advancing years had caused them to withdraw from activity to the shelter of their home — isolated, detached, shut out from the mainstream of daily life and association.

I felt the unmistakable prompting to park my car and visit Ben and Emily, even though I was on the way to a meeting. It was a sunny weekday afternoon. I approached the door to their home and knocked. Emily answered. When she recognized me, her bishop, she exclaimed, "All day long I have waited for my phone to ring. It has been silent. I hoped that the postman would deliver a letter. He brought only bills. Bishop, how did you know today was my birthday?"

I answered, "God knows, Emily, for He loves you."

In the quiet of the living room, I said to Ben and Emily, "I don't know why I was directed here today, but our Heavenly Father knows. Let's kneel in prayer and ask Him why." This we did, and the answer came. Emily was asked to sing in the choir, even to provide a solo for the forthcoming ward conference. Ben was asked to speak to the Aaronic Priesthood young men and recount a special experience in his life when his safety was assured by responding to the promptings of the Spirit. She sang. He spoke. Hearts were gladdened by the return to activity of Ben and Emily. They rarely missed a sacrament meeting from that day to the time each was called home. The language of the Spirit had been spoken. It had been heard. It had been understood. Hearts were touched and lives saved.

Second, the gratitude of God for a life well lived.

For my second example I turn to the release of a stake

president in Star Valley, Wyoming, the late E. Francis Winters. He had served faithfully for the lengthy term of twenty-three years. Though modest by nature and circumstance, he had been a perpetual pillar of strength to everyone in the valley. On the day of the stake conference, the building was filled to overflowing. Each heart seemed to be saying a silent "thank you" to this noble leader who had given so unselfishly of his life for the benefit of others.

As I stood to speak following the reorganization of the stake presidency, I was prompted to respond in a manner totally new to me. I stated how long Francis Winters had presided in the stake; then I asked all whom he had blessed or confirmed as children to stand and remain standing. Next I asked all those persons whom President Winters had ordained, set apart, personally counseled, or blessed to please stand. The result was electrifying. Every person in the audience stood. Tears flowed freely, tears that communicated better than could words the gratitude of tender hearts. I turned to President and Sister Winters and said, "We are witnesses today of the prompting of the Spirit. This vast throng reflects not only individual feelings but also the gratitude of God for a life well lived."

Third, the knowledge that we do not walk alone.

Stan, a dear friend of mine, was stricken by cancer. He had been robust in health, athletic in build, and active in many pursuits. Now he was unable to walk or to stand. His wheelchair was his home. The finest of physicians had cared for him, and the prayers of family and friends had been offered in a spirit of hope and trust. Yet Stan continued to lie in the confinement of his bed at University Hospital.

Late one afternoon I was swimming at Deseret Gym, gazing at the ceiling while backstroking width after width.

61

Silently, but ever so clearly, there came to my mind the thought: "Here you swim almost effortlessly, while your friend Stan is unable to move." I felt the prompting: "Get to the hospital and give him a blessing."

I ceased my swimming, dressed, and hurried to Stan's room at the hospital. His bed was empty. A nurse said he was in his wheelchair at the swimming pool, preparing for therapy. I hurried to the area, and there was Stan, all alone, at the edge of the deeper portion of the pool. We greeted each other and returned to his room, where a priesthood blessing was provided.

Slowly but surely, strength and movement returned to Stan's legs. First he could stand on faltering feet. Then he learned once again to walk, step by step. Today one would not know that Stan had lain so close to death and with no hope of recovery.

Frequently Stan speaks in church meetings and tells of the goodness of the Lord to him. To some he reveals the dark thoughts of depression that engulfed him that afternoon as he sat in his wheelchair at the edge of the pool, sentenced, it seemed, to a life of despair. He tells how he pondered the alternative. It would be so easy to propel the hated wheelchair into the silent water of the deep pool. Life would then be over. But at that precise moment he saw me, his friend. That day Stan learned literally that we do not walk alone. I too learned a lesson that day: never, never, never postpone a prompting.

Later, as Stan's youngest son was married for all eternity and the family had assembled in the sacred temple of the Lord, we paused and remembered the miracle we had witnessed. Words did not come easily from emotion-filled hearts, but a silent chorus of gratitude spoke the feelings that words were inadequate to express.

As we pursue the journey of life, let us learn the language of the Spirit. May we always remember and respond to the Master's gentle invitation: "Behold, I stand at the door, and knock: if any man hear my voice, and open the door, I will come in to him." (Revelation 3:20.) This is the language of the Spirit. He spoke it. He taught it. He lived it. May each of us do likewise.

9

Courage Counts

More than thirty years ago, when I was serving as a bishop, the general session of our stake conference was held in the Assembly Hall on Temple Square in Salt Lake City. Our stake presidency was to be reorganized at that session. Members of the Aaronic Priesthood, including bishops and their counselors, were providing the music for the conference. At the conclusion of our first selection, President Joseph Fielding Smith, our conference visitor, stepped to the pulpit and read for sustaining approval the names of the new stake presidency. I am confident the other members of the stake presidency had been made aware of their callings, but I had not. After reading my name, President Smith announced: "If Brother Monson is willing to respond to this call, we shall be pleased to hear from him now."

As I stood at the pulpit and gazed out on that sea of faces, I remembered the song we had just sung. Its title was "Have Courage, My Boy, to Say No." That day I selected as my acceptance theme "Have Courage, My Boy, to Say Yes." I learned, in a most vivid and dramatic manner, the truth that *courage counts.*

Life's journey is not traveled on a freeway devoid of obstacles, pitfalls, and snares. Rather, it is a pathway marked by forks and turnings. Decisions are constantly before us. To make them wisely, courage is needed: the courage to say no, the courage to say yes. Decisions do determine destiny.

The call for courage comes constantly to each of us. It has ever been so, and so shall it ever be. The battlefields of war witness acts of courage. Some are printed on pages of books or contained on rolls of film, while others are indelibly impressed on the human heart.

The courage of a military leader was recorded by a young infantryman wearing the gray uniform of the Confederacy during America's Civil War. He described the influence of General J. E. B. Stuart in these words: "At a critical point in the battle, he leaped his horse over the breastworks near my company, and when he had reached a point about the center of the brigade, while the men were loudly cheering him, he waved his hand toward the enemy and shouted, 'Forward men. Forward! Just follow me!' The men were wild with enthusiasm. With courage and resolution, they poured over the breastworks after him like a raging torrent, and the objective was seized and held." (Emory M. Thomas, *Bold Dragoon: The Life of J. E. B. Stuart* [New York: Harper & Row, 1986].)

At an earlier time, and in a land far distant, another leader issued the same plea, "Follow me." He was not a general of war. Rather, He was the Prince of peace, the Son of God. Those who followed Him then, and those who follow Him now, may win a far more significant victory, with consequences that are everlasting. But the need for courage is constant. Courage is ever required.

The holy scriptures portray the evidence of this truth. Joseph, son of Jacob, the same who was sold into Egypt, demonstrated the firm resolve of courage when to Potiphar's wife, who attempted to seduce him, he declared: "How . . .

can I do this great wickedness, and sin against God? And . . . [Joseph] hearkened not unto her, . . . and got . . . out." (Genesis 39:9-10, 12.)

In our day, a father applied this example of courage to the lives of his children by declaring: "If you ever find yourself where you shouldn't ought to be — get out!"

The prophet Daniel demonstrated supreme courage by standing up for what he knew to be right and by demonstrating the courage to pray, though threatened by death were he to do so. (See Daniel 6.)

Courage characterized the life of Abinadi, as shown in the Book of Mormon by his willingness to offer his life rather than deny the truth. (See Mosiah 13:1-9; 17:5-20.)

Who can help but be inspired by the lives of the two thousand stripling sons of Helaman, who taught and demonstrated the need for courage to follow the teachings of parents, the courage to be chaste and pure? (See Alma 56.)

Perhaps each of these accounts is crowned by the example of Moroni, who had the courage to persevere to the end in righteousness.

All were fortified by the words of Moses: "Be strong and of a good courage, fear not, nor be afraid: . . . for the Lord thy God, he it is that doth go with thee; he will not fail thee, nor forsake thee." (Deuteronomy 31:6.)

He did not fail them. He will not fail us. He did not forsake them. He will not forsake us.

It was this knowledge that prompted the courage of Columbus, the quiet resolve to record in his ship's log again and again: "This day we sailed on." It was this witness that motivated the Prophet Joseph Smith to declare, "I am going like a lamb to the slaughter; but I am calm as a summer's morning." (D&C 135:4.)

It is this sweet assurance that can guide you and me — in our time, in our day, in our lives. Of course we will face fear, experience ridicule, and meet opposition. Let us have the courage to defy the consensus, the courage to stand for principle. Courage, not compromise, brings the smile of God's approval. Courage becomes a living and an attractive virtue when it is regarded not only as a willingness to die manfully, but also as the determination to live decently. A moral coward is one who is afraid to do what he thinks is right because others will disapprove or laugh. Remember that all men have their fears, but those who face their fears with dignity have courage as well.

From my personal chronology of courage, let me share with you two examples, one from military service, one from missionary experience.

Entering the United States Navy in the closing months of World War II was a challenging experience for me. I learned of brave deeds, acts of valor, and examples of courage. One best remembered was the quiet courage of an eighteen-year-old seaman, not of our faith, who was not too proud to pray. Of two hundred and fifty men in the company, he was the only one who each night knelt down by the side of his bunk, at times amidst the jeers of the curious, the jests of unbelievers, and, with bowed head, prayed to God. He never wavered. He never faltered. He had courage.

Missionary service has ever called for courage. One who responded to this call was Randall Ellsworth. While serving in Guatemala as a missionary for The Church of Jesus Christ of Latter-day Saints, Elder Ellsworth survived a devastating earthquake that hurled a beam down on his back, paralyzing his legs and severely damaging his kidneys. He was the only

American injured in the quake, which claimed the lives of some eighteen thousand persons.

After receiving emergency medical treatment, Randall was flown to a large hospital near his home in Rockville, Maryland. While he was confined there, a newscaster conducted with him an interview that I witnessed through the miracle of television. The reporter asked, "Can you walk?"

The answer, "Not yet, but I will."

"Do you think you will be able to complete your mission?"

Came the reply, "Others think not, but I will. With the president of my church praying for me, and through the prayers of my family, my friends, and my missionary companions, I will walk and I will return to Guatemala. The Lord wants me to preach the gospel there for two years, and that's what I intend to do."

There followed a lengthy period of therapy, punctuated by heroic yet silent courage. Little by little, feeling began to return to the almost lifeless limbs. More therapy, more courage, more prayer. At last, Randall Ellsworth walked aboard the plane that carried him back to the mission to which he had been called, back to the people he loved. Behind he left a trail of skeptics, a host of doubters, but also hundreds amazed at the power of God, the miracle of faith, and the example of courage.

On his return to Guatemala, Randall Ellsworth supported himself with the help of two canes. His walk was slow and deliberate. Then one day, as he stood before his mission president, Elder Ellsworth heard these almost unbelievable words spoken to him: "You have been the recipient of a miracle," said the mission president. "Your faith has been rewarded. If you have the necessary confidence, if you have abiding faith, if you have supreme courage, place those two canes on my desk and walk."

After a long pause, first one cane and then the other was placed on the desk, and a missionary walked. It was halting, it was painful—but he walked, never again to need the canes.

Recently I thought once more of the courage demonstrated by Randall Ellsworth. Years had passed since his ordeal. He was now a husband and a father. An engraved announcement arrived at my office. It read: "The President and Directors of Georgetown University announce commencement exercises of Georgetown University School of Medicine." Randall Ellsworth received his doctor of medicine degree. More effort, more study, more faith, more sacrifice, more courage had been required. The price was paid, the victory won.

Let us be active participants, not mere spectators, on the stage of priesthood power. May we muster courage at the crossroads, courage for the conflicts, courage to say no, courage to say yes, for *courage counts.*

10

The Doorway of Love

Recently there moved over the wires of Associated Press a catalog of crime as the daily happenings around the world were relayed to the media and thence to homes on every continent.

The headlines were brief, but they highlighted murder, rape, robbery, molestation, fraud, deceit, and corruption. I made note of several: "Man slays wife and children, then turns gun on self." "Child identifies molester." "Hundreds lose all as multimillion dollar scam is exposed." The sordid list continued. Shades of Sodom, glimpses of Gomorrah.

President Ezra Taft Benson has often stated: "We live in a wicked world." The Apostle Paul warned: "Men shall be lovers of their own selves, covetous, boasters, proud, blasphemers, disobedient to parents, unthankful, unholy, . . . lovers of pleasures more than lovers of God." (2 Timothy 3:2, 4.)

Must we suffer the same fate as those who lived in the cities of the plain? Can we not learn the lesson taught in the time of Noah? "Is there no balm in Gilead?" (Jeremiah 8:22.) Or is there a doorway that leads us from the morass of worldliness onward and upward to the high ground of righteousness? There echoes ever so gently to the honest mind that personal invitation of the Lord: "Behold, I stand at the door, and knock: if any man hear my voice, and open the door, I will come in to him." (Revelation 3:20.) Does that doorway have a name? It surely does. I have chosen to call it "The Doorway of Love."

Love is the catalyst that causes change. Love is the balm that brings healing to the soul. But love doesn't grow like weeds or fall like rain. Love has its price. "God so loved the world, that he gave his only begotten Son, that whosoever believeth in him should not perish, but have everlasting life." (John 3:16.) That Son, even the Lord Jesus Christ, gave His life that we might have eternal life, so great was His love for His Father and for us.

In that tender and touching farewell, as He counseled His beloved disciples, Jesus taught: "He that hath my commandments, and keepeth them, he it is that loveth me." (John 14:21.) Particularly far reaching was the instruction, "A new commandment I give unto you, That ye love one another; as I have loved you, that ye also love one another." (John 13:34.)

Little children can learn the lesson of love. While profound instruction from holy writ ofttimes is not understood by them, they respond readily to a favorite verse:

> "I love you, Mother," said little John;
> Then, forgetting his work, his cap went on
> And he was off to the garden swing,
> Leaving her the water and wood to bring.

> "I love you, Mother," said rosy Nell.
> "I love you better than tongue can tell."
> Then she teased and pouted full half the day
> Till her mother rejoiced when she went to play.

72

"I love you, Mother," said little Fan.
"Today I'll help you all I can.
How glad I am that school doesn't keep."
So she rocked the baby till it fell asleep.

Then, stepping softly, she fetched the broom
And swept the floor and tidied the room.
Busy and happy all day was she,
Helpful and happy as a child could be.

"I love you, Mother," again they said,
Three little children going to bed.
How do you think that Mother guessed
Which of them really loved her best?

Home should be a haven of love. Honor, courtesy, and respect symbolize love and characterize the righteous family. Fathers in such homes will not hear the denunciation of the Lord as recorded in the book of Jacob from the Book of Mormon: "Ye have broken the hearts of your tender wives, and lost the confidence of your children, because of your bad examples before them; and the sobbings of their hearts ascend up to God against you." (Jacob 2:35.)

In Third Nephi the Master instructed us: "There shall be no disputations among you. . . . For verily, verily I say unto you, he that hath the spirit of contention is not of me, but is of the devil, who is the father of contention, and he stirreth up the hearts of men to contend with anger, one with another. Behold, this is not my doctrine, to stir up the hearts of men with anger, one against another; but this is my doctrine, that such things should be done away." (3 Nephi 11:28-30.)

Where love is, there is no disputation. Where love is, there is no contention. Where love is, there God will be also. Each of us has the responsibility to keep His commandments. The lessons found in scripture find fulfillment in our lives. Joseph Smith taught that "happiness is the object and design of our existence; and will be the end thereof, if we pursue the path that leads to it; and this path is virtue, uprightness, faithfulness, holiness, and keeping all the commandments of God." (*Teachings of the Prophet Joseph Smith,* pp. 255-56.)

In the classic musical production *Camelot,* there is a line with words of warning for all. After the familiar triangle began to deepen regarding King Arthur, Lancelot, and Guenevere, King Arthur said, "We must not let our passions destroy our dreams."

From that same production came another truth also spoken by Arthur as he envisioned a better world: "Violence is not strength, and compassion is not weakness."

In this world in which we live, there is a tendency for us to describe needed change, required help, and desired relief with the familiar phrase, "They ought to do something about this." We fail to define the word *they.* I love the message: "Let there be peace on earth, and let it begin with me." Tears came to my eyes when I read of a young boy in one of our eastern cities who noticed a vagrant asleep on a sidewalk and who then went to his own bedroom, retrieved his pillow, and placed it beneath the head of that one whom he knew not. Perhaps there came from the past these welcome words: "Inasmuch as ye have done it unto one of the least of these my brethren, ye have done it unto me." (Matthew 25:40.)

I extol those who, with loving care and compassionate concern, feed the hungry, clothe the naked, and house the homeless. He who notes the sparrow's fall will not be unmindful of such service.

The desire to lift, the willingness to help, and the graciousness to give come from a heart filled with love. Somehow the memory of mother prompts such loving concern.

Some years ago there passed from mortality a friend who helped more people, spoke more eulogies, and gave more freely of his time, his talents, and his possessions than most. His name was Louis. He related to me this tender account:

A gentle, soft-spoken mother had passed away. She left to her stalwart sons and lovely daughters no fortune of finance but, rather, a heritage of wealth in example, in sacrifice, in obedience. After the funeral eulogies had been spoken and the sad trek to the cemetery had been made, the grown family sorted through the meager possessions the mother had left. Louis discovered a note and also a key. The note instructed: "In the corner bedroom, in the bottom drawer of my dresser, is a tiny box. It contains the treasure of my heart. This key will open the box." Another son asked, "What could Mother have of sufficient value to be placed under lock and key?" A sister commented, "Dad has been gone all these years, and Mother has had precious little of this world's goods."

The box was removed from its resting place in the dresser drawer and opened carefully with the aid of the key. What did it contain? No money, no deed, no precious rings or valuable jewels. Louis took from the box a faded photograph of his father. On the back of the photograph was the penned message, "My dear husband and I were sealed together for time and all eternity in the House of the Lord, at Salt Lake City, December 12, 1891."

Next there emerged an individual photo of each child, with his or her name and birthdate. Finally, Louis held to the light a homemade valentine. In crude, childlike penmanship, which he recognized as his own, Louis read the words he had written sixty years before: "Dear Mother, I love you."

Hearts were tender, voices soft, and eyes moist. Mother's treasure was her eternal family. Its strength rested on the bedrock foundation of "I love you."

A poet wrote, "Love is the most noble attribute of the human soul." A schoolteacher showed her love with her guiding philosophy: "No one fails in my class. I have the responsibility to help each student succeed."

A priesthood quorum leader in Salt Lake City, a retired executive, said to me, "This year I have helped twelve of my brethren who were out of work to obtain permanent employment. I have never been happier in my entire life." Short in stature, "Little Ed," as we affectionately called him, stood tall that day as his eyes glistened and his voice quavered. He showed his love by helping those in need.

A large and tough businessman, a wholesale vendor of poultry, showed his love with a single comment made when a customer attempted to pay for twenty-four roasting chickens. "The chickens are going to the widows, aren't they? There will be no charge." Then he added in a faltering voice, "And there are more where these came from."

A few years ago Morgan High School played Millard High for the Utah State football championship. From his wheelchair, to which he was confined, Morgan coach Jan Smith said to his team, "This is the most important game of your lives. You lose, and you will regret it forever. You win, and you will remember it forever. Make every play as though it were all-important."

Behind the door, his wife, to whom he tenderly referred as his chief assistant, overheard her husband say, "I love you guys. I don't care about the ball game. I love you and want the game victory for you." Underdog Morgan High won the football game and the state championship.

The Doorway of Love

True love is a reflection of Christ's love. In December of each year we call it the Christmas spirit. You can hear it. You can see it. You can feel it. But never alone.

One winter day as Christmas approached, I thought back to an experience from my boyhood. I was just eleven. Our Primary president, Melissa, was an older and loving gray-haired lady. One day at Primary, Melissa asked me to stay behind and visit with her. There the two of us sat in the otherwise empty chapel. She placed her arm about my shoulder and began to cry. Surprised, I asked her why she was crying. She replied, "I don't seem to be able to encourage the Trail Builder boys to be reverent during the opening exercises of Primary. Would you be willing to help me, Tommy?" I promised her I would. Strangely to me, but not to Melissa, that ended any problem of reverence in that Primary. She had gone to the source of the problem—me. The solution was love.

The years flew by. Marvelous Melissa, now in her nineties, lived in a nursing facility in the northwest part of Salt Lake City. Just before Christmas I determined to visit my beloved Primary president. Over the car radio, I heard the song "Hark! the Herald Angels Sing." I reflected on the visit made by wise men those long years ago. They brought gifts of gold, of frankincense, and of myrrh. I brought only the gift of love and a desire to say "Thank you."

I found Melissa in the lunchroom. She stared at her plate of food, teasing it with the fork she held in her aged hand. Not a bite did she eat. As I spoke to her, my words were met by a benign but blank stare. I took the fork in hand and began to feed Melissa, talking all the time I did so about her service to boys and girls as a Primary worker. There wasn't so much as a glimmer of recognition, far less a spoken word. Two other residents of the nursing home gazed at me with puzzled expressions. At last they spoke, saying, "She doesn't know anyone, even her own family. She hasn't said a word in all the years she's been here."

Lunch ended. My one-sided conversation wound down. I stood to leave. I held her frail hand in mine, gazed into her wrinkled but beautiful countenance, and said, "God bless you, Melissa. Merry Christmas." Without warning, she spoke the words, "I know you. You're Tommy Monson, my Primary boy. How I love you." She pressed my hand to her lips and bestowed on it the kiss of love. Tears coursed down her cheeks and bathed our clasped hands. Those hands, that day, were hallowed by heaven and graced by God. The herald angels did sing. Outside the sky was blue — azure blue. The air was cool — crispy cool. The snow was white — crystal white. The words of the Master seemed to have a personal meaning never before fully felt: "Woman, behold thy son!" And to his disciple, "Behold thy mother!" (John 19:26-27.)

> How silently, how silently,
> The wondrous gift is giv'n!
> So God imparts to human hearts
> The blessings of his heav'n.
> No ear may hear his coming;
> But in this world of sin,
> Where meek souls will receive him, still
> The dear Christ enters in.
> —Phillips Brooks

The wondrous gift was given, the heavenly blessing was received, the dear Christ had entered in — all through the doorway of love.

11

A Refuge from the Storms of Life

During the Pacific wars of this great nation, the port of Seattle played a most significant role in the lives of servicemen numbering in the millions. As anchors were weighed and mighty vessels slipped silently ever westward, decks were lined with silent and thoughtful men taking one last glance at the land they loved. For many it became a last glance indeed, as war took its dreadful toll.

Seattle was the scene of many homecomings, too. Giant carriers limped there for repairs; then finally the troop ships followed, emptying to a grateful nation their precious cargo of men. "Home was the sailor, home from the sea."

It is fitting that a temple of God now marks this part of our blessed land of freedom. A beacon to all, the temple seems to extend a gentle invitation, "Come, come ye to the House of the Lord." Here His precious plan is taught. Here eternal covenants are made. Here unfailing devotion is pledged. Labors are not confined to self alone, for in this and every temple two twin endeavors go hand in hand: temple work for one's self and temple work for others. Baptisms, endowments, and sacred sealings are performed in behalf of those who have gone beyond, including that throng who, during the dark days of war, waved goodbye to Seattle, never again to return.

As a temple is dedicated, may we also rededicate our lives. The Apostle Paul counseled: "Know ye not that ye are the temple of God, and that the Spirit of God dwelleth in you?" (1 Corinthians 3:16.) When we pattern our lives after the blueprint given through revelation to the Prophet Joseph Smith at Kirtland, Ohio, in December of 1832, we will be fashioning temples prepared for eternity. Spoke the Lord: "Organize yourselves; prepare every needful thing; and establish a house, even a house of prayer, a house of fasting, a house of faith, a house of learning, a house of glory, a house of order, a house of God." (D&C 88:119.) Such houses will withstand the storms and stresses of life and will become celestial dwelling places. Let us ever remember that which we learn in holy temples of God. These teachings have eternal impact.

Some time ago, as the First Presidency and Council of the Twelve met in the upper room of the temple, there came a special prayer at a sacred altar. Remembered were the names of those whom we knew and who, by reason of serious illness, needed divine help. Many of the names were well known, belonging to faithful persons of prominence. Others were less known, but equally as faithful. One name I had placed to be read before the Lord of Hosts was that of a sweet, young wife, a lovely mother, a daughter of God—stricken with a terminal illness. I had not as yet met Karen, but her plight had been conveyed to me, and I was to join her husband early that same evening, that a priesthood blessing might be provided her.

Our temple meeting concluded, the business of the office was transacted, and by late afternoon the Church Administration Building emptied. A quiet peace pervaded the hallways, entered my office, and touched my heart. What would

I say to one so stricken? How might her grief be assuaged? How might hope banish despair and joy replace sorrow? Such were my thoughts as they became part of my personal prayer.

At six I met my guests and bid them be seated in my office. It was obvious they were humble of heart yet undaunted in their faith. It is difficult for one terminally ill to smile, but smile she did, though tears glistened in her eyes. Her voice quavered a bit as she told me of the love she had for her husband, the concern she felt in leaving her children. "They are so young and so need their mother," she pleaded. Karen and her husband looked into my eyes and waited for my response. Unashamedly I confess I felt inadequate to the responsibility. Then I gazed at the two pictures that grace the walls of my office.

I directed my young friends first to the portrait of the Savior. We talked of His life, His love, and His mission. We remembered that He, too, loved little children and was mindful of them. I testified that He would be mindful of her little ones. We reviewed His atoning sacrifice; its pain, its purpose. His words seemed to flow through my mind. I spoke them in reverence. "Peace I leave with you, my peace I give unto you: not as the world giveth, give I unto you. Let not your heart be troubled, neither let it be afraid." (John 14:27.) "In my Father's house are many mansions: if it were not so I would have told you. I go to prepare a place for you . . . that where I am, there ye may be also." (John 14:2-3.)

Turning from the Savior's portrait, we glanced at the other painting — the Master before His disciples, revealing the wounds of His body and portraying the reality of His resurrection. We opened the Bible to Paul's magnificent testimony — his epistle to the Corinthians — and read aloud: "Christ died for our sins according to the scriptures; and . . .

81

he was buried, and . . . arose again the third day. . . . He was seen of Cephas, then of the twelve: after that, he was seen of above five hundred brethren at once. . . . After that, he was seen of James, then of all the apostles. And last of all he was seen of me also, as of one born out of due time." (1 Corinthians 15:3-8.)

We discussed His plan of salvation. Our pre-earth life was mentioned as we recalled Jeremiah's promise: "Before I formed thee . . . I knew thee; and before thou camest forth . . . I sanctified thee, and I ordained thee a prophet unto the nations." (Jeremiah 1:5.)

Next we spoke of earth life, that transient period so brief for some, so long and labored for others. We turned to the Book of Mormon and read Alma's description of Paradise. Oh, the comfort this Book of Mormon prophet provided. As we reviewed the glorious resurrection, our thoughts and our conversation moved inexorably to the temple. The holy endowment was pondered, the sacred sealing at a special altar remembered. "For time and for all eternity" was more than a phrase. It was and is a precious promise.

The hour had grown late. A worthy husband and I blessed a sweet and tender wife and mother who, barring a modern miracle, would soon pass beyond this veil of tears to her heavenly home. Our faith was united, the Lord so close, the experience so sacred.

I escorted my young friends from the building, but not before showing them the beautiful room where the First Presidency meets, where the prophet sits, and where inspired decisions are made. Then they were gone.

Returning to my office, I noticed on the hallway floor a small necklace that had broken and fallen to the carpet. As I picked up Karen's necklace, I thought: How like life is this necklace — lovely in adornment, but so susceptible to damage and risk of loss. I then reflected on the eternal covenant that bound my young friends — an unbreakable bond, even a temple marriage. Children, theirs for all eternity, are part of that sacred sealing.

I darkened the room, but before closing the door I dropped to my knees and thanked my Heavenly Father for holy houses — even temples of the Most High God. The enemy of death has been conquered. Eternal life reigns triumphant — not for Karen alone, but for all whose knees shall bow, whose tongues confess that Jesus is the Christ, and who love Him and keep His commandments. Hear His promise: "I, the Lord, am merciful and gracious unto those who fear me, and delight to honor those who serve me in righteousness and in truth unto the end. Great shall be their reward and eternal shall be their glory." (D&C 76:5-6.)

May such be our experience.

This chapter is adapted from an address delivered at the dedication of the Seattle Temple in November 1980.

12

Guideposts on the Pathway to Perfection

Commencement is a most significant time in our lives. Many years of study culminate in graduation. On this occasion we are sober in thought, serious in attitude, and very much aware that graduation is not the completion of a tedious book, but simply the ending of one chapter and the beginning of another in our exciting book of life.

And what an exciting life awaits us. We may not be a John Cabot, sailing off into the blue with the king's patent to discover new lands, nor a Captain James Cook, who declared, "I had ambition not only to go farther than any man had ever been before, but as far as it was possible for a man to go."

But we can be explorers in spirit, with a mandate to make this world better by discovering improved ways of living and of doing things. The spirit of exploration, whether it be of the surface of the earth, the vastness of space, or the principles of living greatly, includes developing the capacity to face trouble with courage, disappointment with cheerfulness, and triumph with humility.

Carl Sandburg described our possibilities: "I see America, not in the setting sun of a black night of despair ahead of us. I see America in the crimson light of a rising sun, fresh from the burning creative hand of God. I see great days ahead, great days possible to men and women of will and vision."

However, during the last half century, there has been in the United States a gradual but continual retreat from standards of excellence in many phases of our life. We observe business without morality; science without humanity; knowledge without character; worship without sacrifice; pleasure without conscience; politics without principle; and wealth without works.

Perhaps the renowned author Charles Dickens, without really realizing his prophetic powers, described our day when he spoke of a period two centuries ago. His classic *A Tale of Two Cities* begins: "It was the best of times, it was the worst of times, it was the age of wisdom, it was the age of foolishness, it was the epoch of belief, it was the epoch of incredulity, it was the season of Light, it was the season of Darkness, it was the spring of hope, it was the winter of despair, we had everything before us, we had nothing before us."

This is the world we enter at commencement. Our future is in our hands. The outcome is up to each of us.

As we commence our journey, we must remember that to measure progress by so-called delights and thrills is to apply a false standard. The pathway to perfection does not feature a glut of luxury. Progress is not synonymous with commercially produced pleasure, the nightclub idea of what is a good time, mistaking it for joy and happiness.

On the contrary, obedience to law, respect for others, mastery of self, and joy in service are the guideposts that mark the pathway to perfection. Perhaps we would best understand these guideposts if we discussed them on an individual basis.

First, *obedience to law.*

We turn at once to that revered and renowned code of conduct that has guided mankind through every conceivable turmoil. In so doing, we seem to hear the echo of the voice from Mount Sinai speaking to us today, here and now:

Thou shalt have no other gods before me.
Thou shalt not make unto thee any graven image.
Thou shalt not take the name of the Lord thy God in vain.
Remember the sabbath day, to keep it holy.
Honor thy father and thy mother.
Thou shalt not kill.
Thou shalt not commit adultery.
Thou shalt not steal.
Thou shalt not bear false witness.
Thou shalt not covet. (See Exodus 20.)

The late Cecil B. DeMille stated, after exhaustive research for the epic motion picture *The Ten Commandments*: "Man can't break the Ten Commandments. He can only break himself against them."

Years after the law of Moses was given, there came the meridian of time, when a great endowment emerged—a power stronger than weapons, a wealth more lasting than the coins of Caesar; for the King of kings and the Lord of lords introduced into the principles of law the concept of love. The Apostle Paul, in his epistle to the Romans, declared: "Let every soul be subject unto the higher powers. For there is no power but of God," and "Love is the fulfilling of the law." (Romans 13:1, 10.)

We must obey the laws of God. Violate them and we suffer lasting consequences. Obey them and we reap everlasting joy.

Let us not overlook obedience to the laws of the land.

They do not restrict our conduct so much as they guarantee our freedom, provide us protection, and safeguard all that is dear to us.

Coming as I do from the world of business, I cannot move on without pausing to mention obedience to the laws — not theories — of economics. One cannot continually spend more than he earns and remain solvent. This law applies to nations as well as to people. A worker cannot, in the long run, adhere to a philosophy of something for nothing as opposed to something for something. Nor can management dismiss as optional the necessity of an adequate corporate profit and a reasonable return to shareholders if our economy of free enterprise is to flourish.

One person of wisdom observed, "Laws are the rules by which the game of life is played." In reality, they are much more: obedience to law is a critical guidepost if we are to proceed to perfection.

Second, *respect for others.*

People, by nature, are tempted to seek their own glory and not the glory of their neighbors or the glory of God. None of us lives alone. There is no dividing line between our prosperity and our neighbor's wretchedness.

Before we can love and respect our neighbors, we must place them in proper perspective. One person said, "I looked at my brother with the microscope of criticism and I said, 'How coarse my brother is.' I looked at my brother with the telescope of scorn and I said, 'How small my brother is.' Then I looked into the mirror of truth and I said, 'How like me my brother is.' "

Respect for others implies a concern and a love for our fellow human beings. Too many have been screaming ever louder for more and more of the things we cannot take with us and paying less and less attention to the real sources of the very happiness we seek. We have been measuring others more by balance sheets and less by moral standards. We have developed frightening physical power and fallen into pathetic spiritual weakness. We have become so concerned over the growth of our earning capacity that we have neglected the growth of our character.

As we view the disillusionment that today engulfs countless thousands, we are learning the hard way what an ancient prophet wrote out for us three thousand years ago: "He that loveth silver shall not be satisfied with silver; nor he that loveth abundance with increase." (Ecclesiastes 5:10.)

It is an immutable law that the more you give away, the more you receive. You make a living by what you get, but you make a life by what you give.

Happiness abounds when there is genuine respect one for another. Wives draw closer to their husbands and husbands are more appreciative of their wives; and children are happy, as children are meant to be. Where there is respect in the home, children do not find themselves in that dreaded never-never land — never the object of concern, never the recipient of proper parental guidance.

To those who are not yet married, I counsel: People who marry in the hope of forming a permanent partnership require certain skills and attitudes of mind. They must be skillful in adapting to each other. They need capacity to work out mutual problems. They need willingness to give and take in the search for harmony. They need unselfishness of the highest sort, with thought for one's partner taking the place of desire for oneself.

May I mention an example. Many years ago I had the opportunity to deliver a commencement address to a graduation class of Brigham Young University. I had gone to the home of President Hugh B. Brown, that we might together drive to the university, where he was to conduct the exercises and I was to speak. As President Brown entered my car, he said, "Wait a moment." He looked toward the large bay window of his lovely home, and then I saw what he was looking for. The curtains parted, and I saw Sister Brown, his beloved companion of well over fifty years, at the window, propped up in a wheelchair, waving a little white handkerchief. President Brown took from his inside coat pocket a white handkerchief, which he waved to her in return. Then he turned to me with a smile and said, "Let's go."

I asked President Brown to tell me about the sign of the white handkerchiefs. He related to me the following incident: "The first day after Sister Brown and I were married, as I went to work, I heard a tap at the window, and there she was, waving a handkerchief. I found mine and waved in reply. From that day until this I have never left my home without that little exchange between my wife and me. It is a symbol of our love one for another. It is an indication to one another that all will be well until we are joined together at eventide." This is respect—a vital guidepost on our journey.

Third, *mastery of self.*

Perhaps the surest test of an individual's integrity is his or her refusal to do or say anything that would damage self-respect. The cornerstone of such a person's value system is never "What will others think?," but rather, "What will I think of myself?"

One teacher commented, "In the last analysis, I have to be true to myself. But it is a little tough to do that when I am being false to my students, because I'm a teacher, not for my sake but for the sake of my students. And if I do them any mental, physical, emotional, or social harm, then I drag them down with me into what ought to be, but cannot be, my own private purgatory."

Remembered is this truth: "The power to lead is also the power to mislead, and the power to mislead is the power to destroy." Self-mastery is a rigorous process at best; too many of us want it to be effortless and painless.

Some spurn effort, and substitute an alibi. We hear the plea, "I was denied the advantages others had in their youth." And then we remember the caption that a cartoonist placed under a sketch of Abraham Lincoln's log cabin: "Ill-housed, ill-fed, ill-clothed."

Others say, "I am physically limited." History is replete with successful persons who possessed physical limitations.

Should temporary setbacks afflict us, a very significant part of our struggle for self-mastery is the determination and the courage to try again. Most of us will need that second effort as we pursue life's journey. In the words of the fight song of a high school in Yonkers, New York: "Lead us, oh lead us, Great Moulder of men; / Out of the darkness to strive once again."

The world moves at an increasingly rapid pace. Scientific achievements are fantastic, advances in medicine are phenomenal, and the probings of the inner secrets of earth and the outer limits of space leave one amazed and in awe. In our science-oriented age we conquer space, but we cannot control self; hence, we forfeit peace. Through modern science, man has been permitted to fly through space at undreamed-of speeds and to silently and without effort cruise sixty days underwater in nuclear-powered ships. However, while man can devise the most complex machines to achieve such fan-

91

tastic feats, he cannot give them life or bestow upon them the powers of reason and judgment.

Why? Because these are divine gifts, bestowed solely at God's discretion. God gave man life, and with it the power to think and reason and decide and love. With such power given to you and to me, mastery of self becomes a necessity if we are to have the abundant life.

Fourth, *joy in service.*

To find real happiness, we must seek for it in a focus outside ourselves. No one learns the meaning of living without surrendering ego to the service of others. Service to others is akin to duty, the fulfillment of which brings true joy.

Describing the joy of fulfillment of duty and service to God and country, Sir Winston Churchill, upon the unconditional surrender of enemy forces during World War II, declared: "Weary and worn, impoverished but undaunted and now triumphant, we had a moment that was sublime. We gave thanks to God for the noblest of all His blessings — the sense we had done our duty."

The mantle of leadership is not the cloak of comfort, but the robe of responsibility. Some time ago at our nation's Capitol in Washington, D. C., I had the privilege of addressing a conference of America's religious leaders. My topic — Church welfare services and the response to the Teton Dam disaster in Rexburg, Idaho.

June 5, 1976, was a time of terror for residents of that community, but during that perilous period the people there experienced perhaps their finest hour. Who can forget the outpouring of good will and the service extended by others. Food was provided, shelter erected, clothing donated, love extended. The caravans of electricians, mechanics, and honest laborers, both men and women, who traveled all night to aid those whom they had never met must be recorded as a noble example of service to others.

This is the joy that comes through service.

May we ever look backward with pride and press forward with hope. Our training, our experience, our knowledge are tools to be skillfully used. They have been self-acquired. Our conscience, our love, our faith are delicate and precious instruments to guide our destiny. They have been God-given.

One may ask, "Is there a safe way for me to walk through this world of uncertainty and infinite challenge?" I answer in the words of Louise Haskins, who wrote, "I said to the man who stood at the gate of the year: 'Give me a light that I may tread safely into the unknown.' And he replied, 'Go out into the darkness and put your hand into the hand of God. That shall be to you better than a light and safer than a known way.' "

I bear witness to the truth of this advice. May each of us recognize and follow the guideposts that mark the pathway to perfection—obedience to law, respect for others, mastery of self, and joy in service.

This chapter has been adapted from a baccalaureate address delivered at Ricks College in Rexburg, Idaho, April 2, 1982.

13

Your Journey to Eternal Joy

In a classic poem, author Henry Wadsworth Longfellow described youth and the future. He wrote:

> How beautiful is youth! how bright it gleams
> With its illusions, aspirations, dreams!
> Book of Beginnings, Story without End,
> Each maid a heroine, and each man a friend!

At the dedication of the Idaho Falls Temple, the First Presidency, in the dedicatory prayer, stated: "How glorious and near to the angels is youth that is clean. This youth will have joy unspeakable here and eternal happiness hereafter."

Contemplating the decisions that young people must make, and how their very lives depend on those decisions, I turn to the scriptures for inspiration. A particular word stands out time and time again. The word is *come*. The Lord said, "Come unto me." He said, "Come learn of me." He also said, "Come, follow me." I like that word, *come*. My plea is that we would come to the Lord.

May I provide some suggestions to help young people come unto the Lord, to come and follow Him, to have a code of conduct to influence their decisions, to guide their pathway

95

through mortality, and to ensure that they receive, at the conclusion of life's mission, that salutation, "Well done, good and faithful servant; . . . enter thou into the joy of thy lord." (Matthew 25:23.)

I have divided my code of conduct into four parts:

1. You have a heritage; honor it.
2. You will meet sin; shun it.
3. You have the truth; live it.
4. You have a testimony; share it.

First, you have a heritage; honor it.

There comes thundering to our ears the words from Mount Sinai: "Honour thy father and thy mother." (Exodus 20:12.) Oh, how our parents love us, how they pray for us! I know that parents are praying for our welfare every morning and every night. We must honor them. How do we do that? We can follow them and pattern our lives after theirs.

An example of honoring one's mother took place in a human drama in Salt Lake City. Ruth Fawson, mother of six, had just undergone life-threatening surgery. Her devoted husband and her three sons and three daughters were all at the hospital. The physicians and nurses explained to the family that they could return to their homes and that the staff was prepared to adequately care for Sister Fawson. The family expressed thanks to the hospital staff but indicated a desire for one of their number to be present with their mother, each taking a turn. One of her daughters, Lynne, expressed the feelings of all: "We wanted to be here when Mother awakened and stretched forth her hand, so that it would be our hands she would grasp; it would be our smiles she would see; it would be our words she would hear; it would be our love she would feel."

One of the most popular musicals of our time is *Fiddler on the Roof,* by Joseph Stein. One laughs as the old-fashioned father of a Jewish family in Russia attempts to cope with the changing times, which are brought forcibly home to him by his beautiful daughters. With abandon they sing "Matchmaker, Matchmaker, Make Me a Match." Tevye, the father, replies with "If I Were a Rich Man." Tears come to the our eyes as we hear the beautiful strains of "Sunrise, Sunset," and we appreciate Tevye's love of his native village when the cast sings "Anatevka."

The gaiety of the dance, the rhythm of the music, the excellence of the acting all fade in significance when Tevye speaks what to me becomes the message of the musical. He gathers his lovely daughters to his side and, in the simplicity of his peasant surroundings, counsels them as they ponder their future. "Remember," cautions Tevye, "in Anatevka each of us knows who we are and what God expects us to become."

Contemplating our earthly life, could not each of us well consider Tevye's statement and respond, "Here, each of us knows who we are and what God expects us to become."

Some time ago I had an assignment in St. George, Utah. While there, Sister Monson and I drove to the little cemetery in the nearby community of Santa Clara. We saw many Swiss names on the tombstones: Gubler, Hafen, Stucki. Most of the tombstones were old and weathered. Many of them marked the graves of children. We contemplated how difficult it was for the early pioneers to provide nourishment and sustenance for their families. Children by the score passed away. I pictured mothers and fathers standing by open graves. I thought of the words I read on one tombstone: "A light from our household is gone; a voice we knew is stilled. A place is vacant in our hearts that never can be filled."

We must not wait until that light from our household is gone, until that voice we know is stilled, before we say, "I love you, Mother. I love you, Father." Now is a time to think and a time to thank. May we do both.

Second, you will meet sin; shun it.

Remember these words from the Book of Mormon: "Wickedness never was happiness." (Alma 41:12.)

I recall attending a meeting where President David O. McKay, at that time a counselor in the First Presidency, was speaking. He said, "I implore you to think clean thoughts." He then made this significant declaration of truth: "Every action is preceded by a thought. If we want to control our actions, we must control our thinking." That is a profound statement of truth. If we fill our minds with good thoughts, our actions will be proper. May we be able to echo in truth the line from Tennyson spoken by Sir Galahad: "My strength is as the strength of ten because my heart is pure."

Essential to success and happiness is the advice, "Choose your friends with caution." In a survey made in selected wards and stakes of the Church, we learned a most significant fact. Those persons whose friends married in the temple usually married in the temple, while those whose friends did not marry in the temple usually did not themselves marry in the temple. The influence of one's friends appeared to be a more dominant factor than parental urging, classroom instruction, or proximity to a temple.

We tend to become like those whom we admire. As in Nathaniel Hawthorne's classic story "The Great Stone Face," we adopt the mannerisms, the attitudes, even the conduct of those whom we admire—and they are usually our friends. We should associate with those who, like us, are planning not for temporary convenience, shallow goals, or narrow ambition, but for those things that matter most—even eternal objectives.

Inscribed on the wall of Stanford University Memorial Hall is this truth: "We must teach our youth that all that is not eternal is too short, and all that is not infinite is too small."

Beyond the friends of our peer group, even our own age, will we make a friend of our father? Each of us actually has three fathers. First, we have our Heavenly Father. He stands ready to answer the prayers of our heart. Being the Father of our spirits, and having created us in His own image, He knows the end from the beginning; His wisdom faileth not and His counsel is ever true. Make a friend of Him.

Each of us also has an earthly father. He labors to insure our happiness. Together with our mother, he prays for our guidance and well-being. Make a friend of him.

Our third father is the father of our ward, even the bishop. He has been called of God by prophecy and the laying on of hands, by those who are in authority, to preach the gospel and administer in the ordinances thereof. In short, he is endowed to provide us with counsel and help. Make a friend of him.

These, our true friends and fathers, will strengthen us constantly.

Third, you have the truth; live it.

The Apostle Paul said to Timothy, "Let no man despise thy youth; but be thou an example of the believers." (1 Timothy 4:12.) President Stephen L Richards was a profound thinker. He said: "Faith and doubt cannot exist in the same mind at the same time, for one will dispel the other." My advice is to seek faith and dispel doubt.

The Lord said: "Seek ye out of the best books words of

wisdom; seek learning, even by study and also by faith." (D&C 88:118.)

> Books are keys to wisdom's treasure;
> Books are gates to lands of pleasure;
> Books are paths that upward lead;
> Books are friends; come, let us read.

Reading is one of the true pleasures of life. In our age of mass culture, when so much that we encounter is abridged, adapted, adulterated, shredded, and boiled down, and commercialism's loudspeakers are incessantly braying, it is mind-easing and mind-inspiring to sit down privately with a good book. It is ennobling when that book contains the revealed word of God.

I think of the words of President J. Reuben Clark, one with whom I had the privilege of associating closely. He said: "You do not find truth groveling through error. You find truth by seeking truth." We can find truth in the standard works of the Church, the teachings of the prophets, the teachings of our parents, and the inspiration that comes to us as we bend our knees and seek the help of God.

We must be true to our ideals, for "ideals are like the stars: you can't touch them with your hands, but by following them you reach your destination."

In pursuit of academic goals, our young people will meet many teachers. I would hope each of those teachers would meet the description written of one: "She created in her room an atmosphere where warmth and acceptance weave their magic spell; where growth and learning, the soaring of the imagination, and the spirit of the young are assured." Unfortunately, there are exceptions to such teachers. There are those who delight to destroy faith rather than build bridges to the good life.

In the words of President J. Reuben Clark: "He wounds, maims, and cripples a soul who raises doubts about or destroys faith in the ultimate truths. God will hold such an one strictly accountable; and who can measure the depths to which one shall fall who fitfully shatters in another the opportunity for celestial glory?"

Since we cannot control the classroom, we can at least prepare the pupil. You ask "How?" I answer: "Provide a guide to the glory of the celestial kingdom of God, even a barometer to distinguish between the truth of God and the theories of men."

Several years ago I held in my hand such a guide. It was a volume of scripture we commonly call the Triple Combination, containing the Book of Mormon, Doctrine and Covenants, and Pearl of Great Price. The book was a gift from a loving father to a beautiful, blossoming daughter who followed carefully his advice. On the flyleaf page her father had written these inspired words, dated April 9, 1944:

> To My Dear Maurine:
> That you may have a constant measure by which to judge between truth and the errors of man's philosophies, and thus grow in spirituality as you increase in knowledge, I give you this sacred book to read frequently and cherish throughout your life.

It was signed "Lovingly your father, Harold B. Lee."

We must never overlook the power of personal prayer. The prayers of a teacher can bring the blessings of heaven to those whom he or she teaches. Consider Sister Hansen, the faithful teacher of a Laurel class in a small mission branch.

How she prayed for inspiration, that she might teach well the precious girls in her class. Particularly did she pray for Betty, a young woman who had been subjected to great stress and temptation to leave the pathway of truth and follow the detour of sin.

Through the constant persuasions of her classmates at school, Betty had decided that she would would attend opening exercises of a special Young Women class, so that she might appear on the roll as being present. Then the sound of an automobile horn would announce to her that her girlfriend and their dates, who were older and far more experienced than Betty, were at hand, and a night of carefully arranged escapade of sin would begin. Then she would be one of the inner circle.

But before calling the roll that night, this humble, loving teacher, Sister Hansen, announced to the class that a shipment from Church headquarters had arrived at her home that day. She had opened the packages and found copies of a pamphlet by Elder Mark E. Petersen. Its subject: chastity. Sister Hansen said, "I feel impressed to leave for another week our lesson scheduled for tonight and want, rather, to review with you the inspiration of this pamphlet. We will each read a paragraph or two aloud, so that all might participate." She looked at each of her precious girls and then said, "Betty, will you begin?" Betty looked at the clock: just two minutes before the scheduled rendezvous. She began to read. Suddenly her heart was touched, her conscience awakened, her determination renewed. She scarcely heard the repeated sound of the automobile horn. She remained throughout the class and rode home with her teacher, her guide, her friend. The temptation to detour from God's approved way had been averted. Satan had been frustrated. A soul had been saved. A prayer had been answered.

Fourth, you have a testimony; share it.

That which we selfishly keep, we lose; but that which we willingly share, we keep. Never underestimate the far-reaching influence of testimony.

One day I congratulated a friend of mine who, together with his wife and family, was preparing to visit the Manti Temple. I asked him to recount to me the experience of his conversion. May I share it with you.

Sharman Hummel and his wife, Anne Marie, lived in the eastern part of the United States and enjoyed a typical American family life with their three lovely daughters. They worked together and they attended their church together, but they had only the most vague idea concerning The Church of Jesus Christ of Latter-day Saints. And then the day came for their lives to change. A transfer of employment came, and Sharman went to the West Coast to prepare for the arrival of his family. The bus ride across the continent was beautiful but rather insignificant until that bus stopped at Salt Lake City. A young woman boarded the bus and sat next to Sharman Hummel. She was en route to Reno to visit an aunt.

Knowing that he was in "Mormon country," Sharman asked the young woman if she were a Mormon. When she answered "Yes," he inquired, "What do you Mormons believe?" The young woman then described what the Church of Jesus Christ meant to her. She mentioned doctrine, but the emphasis was upon testimony and feelings. She described the simplicity of the Church, its teachings, its chapels, its youth program. Said Sharman Hummel, "I don't remember everything she said, but I do remember the spirit in which she said it."

The young woman left the bus at Reno, but all the way to San Francisco, Sharman could think of nothing but what he had learned from this young woman. He immediately investigated the teachings of the gospel; and, through the aid of members and missionaries alike, he, his wife, and their children were converted and baptized.

Sharman Hummel today holds the Melchizedek Priesthood. He has often confided to me that he has but one regret in his life. He never obtained the name of the young woman who sat next to him on the bus and who, in her humble way, taught him what she believed and the importance of acquiring a personal testimony and sharing it. This young woman was prepared. Her spirit gave credence to her testimony. She had been a recipient of the promise of Moroni contained in the Book of Mormon: "And now, I would commend you to seek this Jesus of whom the prophets and apostles have written, that the grace of God the Father, and also the Lord Jesus Christ, and the Holy Ghost, which beareth record of them, may be and abide in you forever." (Ether 12:41.)

Remember that we do not walk alone. The Lord has promised, "I will go before your face. I will be on your right hand and on your left, and my Spirit shall be in your hearts, and mine angels round about you, to bear you up." (D&C 84:88.) As we walk through life, may we always walk toward the light, and the shadows of life will fall behind us.

14

How Do We Show Our Love?

On one occasion an inquiring lawyer came to the Savior and asked, "Master, which is the great commandment in the law?" The Savior responded, "Thou shalt love the Lord thy God with all thy heart, and with all thy soul, and with all thy mind. This is the first and great commandment. And the second is like unto it, Thou shalt love thy neighbour as thyself." (Matthew 22:36-39.)

How do we demonstrate to our Heavenly Father that we love Him? When Sister Monson and I were university students, there was a popular song that had words something like these: "It's easy to say I love you, easy to say I'll be true; easy to say these foolish things, but prove it by the things you do." We have a responsibility to prove to our Heavenly Father, by the things we do, that we love Him.

We demonstrate our love by how well we serve our God. Remember when the Prophet Joseph Smith went to John E. Page and said to him, "Brother Page, you have been called on a mission to Canada."

Brother Page, struggling for an excuse, said, "Brother Joseph, I can't go to Canada. I don't have a coat to wear."

The Prophet took off his own coat, handed it to John Page, and said, "Wear this, and the Lord will bless you."

John Page went on his mission to Canada. In two years he walked something like five thousand miles and baptized six hundred converts. He was successful because he responded to an opportunity to serve his God.

It has been my privilege and pleasure to be on the Church Missionary Committee for many years and to have held in my hand missionary recommendation forms. I remember one on which the bishop had written: "This is the finest young man I have ever recommended for a mission. He was the valedictorian of his high school graduating class, lettered in track and football, was president of his deacons quorum and his teachers quorum, and secretary of the priests quorum. I have not recommended a more outstanding young man." Then he added, "I am proud to be his father."

On another occasion, the bishop had written: "This elder is a very quiet young man. This element of shyness leads an observer to conclude wholesomeness. Although that is not consequential, the conclusion is correct. This elder is a very worthy Latter-day Saint, ready to serve. He has been well trained in manners, etiquette, the gospel, and social graces. He comes from a home where the family continually strives to improve in spiritual strength. He has a testimony of the gospel. He is very sincere, a hard worker. His shyness precludes his displaying the ability he has as a leader. I feel confident that a mission will produce one of the stalwart leaders of the Church in this young man. I highly recommend him for a mission."

Isn't that a beautiful tribute to a young man? The stake president added these comments: "Oldest son in a large family. Clean, alert. His shyness covers a lad with talent and devotion. He is spiritually oriented. Please treat him well, and he will be a great servant of the Lord. He is healthy enough for any assignment. I know of no limitations. Treat him well, train him well, love him as we love him, and the Lord will bless him." These are the finest tributes to a candidate missionary I have ever read. This young man will demonstrate his love of God by how well he serves Him.

We had a missionary in our mission who was particularly devoted and obedient. I said to him one time, "Elder, what is the source of your motivation?"

"Brother Monson," he replied, "I slept in one morning. As I did so, my mind turned to thoughts of my mother and my father, who are operating a little cleaning establishment, working around the clock to earn sufficient money to support me on a mission. As I thought of my parents performing that strenuous work in my behalf, all signs of laziness left me; and I determined that I had an opportunity to serve the Lord in my behalf and in behalf of my own mother and my own father."

Harry Emerson Fosdick said: "Until willingness overflows obligation, men fight as conscripts rather than following the flag as patriots. Duty is never worthily performed until it is performed by one who would gladly do more, if only he could."

In short, we need to extend ourselves in service to our Heavenly Father if we are to demonstrate our love for Him.

I often think of the quiet manner in which President Spencer W. Kimball served his God, without a lot of pomp and ceremony. No one really ever knew all that he did in serving his Heavenly Father, for he did it in the true spirit of the Savior, many times not letting the right hand know what the left was doing. He was the type of man who was willing to put forth any effort the kingdom of God required.

I think also of an account I read about a sweet lady, the

wife of one of our early pioneers. Her name was Catherine Curtis Spencer. She was married to Orson Spencer, a sensitive, well-educated man. Catherine had been reared in Boston and was cultured and refined. She had six children. Her delicate health declined from exposure and hardships after her family was forced to leave Nauvoo. Elder Spencer wrote to her parents and asked if she could return to live with them while he established a home for his family in the West. Their reply: "Let her renounce her degrading faith, and she can come back—but never until she does." Sister Spencer would not renounce her faith. When her parents' letter was read to her, she asked her husband to get his Bible and read to her from the book of Ruth as follows: "Intreat me not to leave thee, or to return from following after thee; for whither thou goest, I will go; and where thou lodgest, I will lodge: thy people shall be my people, and thy God my God." (Ruth 1:16.) Outside the storm raged, the wagon covers leaked, and friends held milk pans over Sister Spencer's head to keep her dry. In these conditions, and without a word of complaint, she closed her eyes for the last time.

This is the spirit of serving God. This is the spirit of putting Him first in our lives. Though we may not necessarily forfeit our lives in service to our God, we can certainly demonstrate our love for Him by how well we serve Him. He who hears our silent prayers, He who observes our unheralded acts will reward us openly when the need comes.

Another example is a family in the mission over which I presided, a family by the name of Agnew. They were difficult people to convert. William Agnew, particularly, would not listen to the missionaries, but finally he consented to attend our Sunday School with his wife, three children, and the two missionaries. However, when the missionaries came on Sunday morning to escort the family to the chapel, there had been a little disagreement in their home. Brother Agnew had insisted, "I will not go to the Mormon Sunday School."

His wife replied, "But you promised, Bill. You promised these young men that you would go."

"I'm not going, and that's that!" he said. He became rather angry, but somewhat reluctantly he permitted his wife and children to go to Sunday School. He later told me of the events of that morning. He said, "When my wife and children shut the door and left me alone in the living room, I had nothing good to say about the Mormon faith. I was about as angry a man as one could imagine. I picked up the morning newspaper to see if I could read about the problems of the world and get my mind off religion, but it was to no avail. I kept thinking, my wife and my children have gone to meet with the Mormons. I then went into my daughter Isabel's bedroom. I thought that perhaps I could turn on the news and hear something different. As I turned on the little radio on her nightstand, what do you think I heard? The Mormon Tabernacle Choir! What message do you think I heard? Richard L. Evans spoke on the subject 'Let Not the Sun Go Down on Thy Wrath.' I felt as though the Lord were talking to me personally. I got down upon my knees and promised my Heavenly Father that I would no longer rail against Him — that I would do what these young missionaries had taught me to do."

When his wife and children returned from Sunday School, they found a new husband and a new father. They couldn't understand why he was in such a pleasant mood. Finally they asked him what had happened to change his attitude.

He said, "I'll tell you. I was so upset when you left that

I read the paper in an attempt to get my mind off all of you. No success. Then I went to Isabel's bedroom and turned on the radio to hear the news, and of all things, I heard the Mormon Tabernacle Choir. This man, Richard Evans, spoke to me and said, 'Don't let the sun go down on thy wrath.' I felt closer to God at that moment than I have ever felt in my life. I am ready to go with you to the meetings. I am ready to pursue a diligent study with the missionaries.''

Isabel said, ''Dad, that's a wonderful story—if only it were true.''

Her father said, ''Isabel, it's true.''

She said, ''No, Dad. Did you say that you turned on the radio on my nightstand?''

He replied, ''That's the one—the little white one.''

''Dad,'' she said, ''that radio hasn't worked for several weeks. I think the tubes are burned out.''

''Isabel,'' he said, ''that radio works. Come with me.'' He led his family into Isabel's bedroom, walked over to the nightstand next to her bed, and turned on the radio as he had done just one hour earlier—but no sound came forth. That radio did not work! But when our Heavenly Father needed to communicate a message to an honest seeker after truth, that radio not only worked, but it tuned him in to the very program and to the very message he needed to bring him to a recognition of the truth. Little wonder that he later became the bishop of that ward. Little wonder that all three of his children are active in the Church and continue to fill positions of responsibility.

When we serve our God, when we love Him, He knows it, and He will take us by the hand and give us answers to our prayers.

''Thou shalt love thy neighbour as thyself.''

Who is my neighbor? Someone asked that question, then answered it: "I don't know his name, but his dog tramples down my flowers. His boy honks the horn and keeps me awake at night, and his children make so much noise I can't enjoy life. But yesterday I noticed some black crepe at his window, and I knew that someone had passed away. I decided it was time I became acquainted with my neighbor."

Let us not wait for that type of event before we become acquainted with our neighbor and show love for him or for her.

Each of us has opportunities for Church assignments. This opportunity of serving in the Church enables us to demonstrate a love of God and a love of our neighbor. It was King Benjamin who said: "When ye are in the service of your fellow beings ye are only in the service of your God." (Mosiah 2:17.) There is no finer way to demonstrate love of God than by serving Him in the positions to which we may be called. Occasionally, the reward for that service will be prompt, and we'll see the light in the eyes of the person whom we have helped. Other times, however, the Lord will let us wait a little while and let our reward come another way. Many are in the process of helping less active people. It is important to never give up, but forever press on in our efforts to help them. The best way to help people to become fully active in the Church is to love them into that activity.

A letter was given to me, written by a young man whose twin brother had been killed while on an activity in Big Cottonwood Canyon east of Salt Lake City. His quorum leader grieved over the loss of one of his boys whom he had been called to serve, to teach, to inspire, and to motivate. He received comfort, as an adviser, in the help our Heavenly Father provided him in the answers to his prayers. He was asked to speak at the funeral of the deceased boy. It was a difficult assignment, but he fulfilled it. Then he received a letter from the surviving twin. The letter is the finest letter he has ever received in mortality. With his permission, I'll share it:

Dear Brother Cannegieter:

I'd like to thank you for the talk you gave at Brian's funeral. You told about all those wonderful times we had with Brian that I had almost forgotten. Brian and I both thought you were the best adviser and the best teacher we ever had, because you really cared about us and gave us your time. You taught us very important lessons and provided us advice from your own experience in life.

We are going to miss Brian very much, and we will never forget the example of living life to its fullest and of courage and of dedication that he gave to us.

I love you, Brother Cannegieter, and I hope I can be as smart and understanding and caring as you are. I hope I will really listen and get to know people like you do.

I'd like to thank you for everything you have done for us.

This is the comfort that comes to the heart of a person who loves his neighbor as himself. The same comfort will come to the heart of the person who loves God.

I attended a stake conference not long ago in Modesto, California, where I was to divide the stake. As I was preparing to do so on Sunday morning, I let my mind go back ten or fifteen years. I remembered that I had previously attended a conference in that area. At that time it was called the Stockton Stake, and Modesto was a unit in that stake. I thought to myself, What was the name of the stake president? Then it came to me; his name was Rooker—Clifton Rooker. I asked the stake presidency as they sat on the stand, "Is this the same stake over which Clifton Rooker presided?"

The brethren said, "Yes, it is. He was our former president."

"It's been many years since I was last here," I said. "Is Brother Rooker here today?"

"Yes, we saw him this morning."

Then I asked, "Where is he seated?"

"We don't rightly know," they replied.

I stepped to the pulpit and asked, "Is Clifton Rooker in the audience?" There he was—way back in the cultural hall. I felt the inspiration to say to him publicly, "Brother Rooker, we have a place for you on the stand. Would you please come forward?" With every eye watching him, Clifton Rooker made that long walk up to the stand and sat by my side. It became my opportunity to call upon him, one of the pioneers of that stake, to bear his testimony—to give him the privilege of telling the people, whom he loved, that he was the real beneficiary of the service he had rendered his Heavenly Father and that he had provided the stake members.

After the session was concluded I said, "Brother Rooker, how would you like to come with me into the high council room and help me set apart the new presidencies of these two stakes?"

He said, "That would be a highlight of my life."

We went into the high council room and, with his hands joining my hands on the head of each person, set apart the two new stake presidencies. We embraced one another as he said goodbye and went to his home.

Can you imagine the shock I received the next morning

when I received a telephone call from his son, who said, "Brother Monson, I'd like to tell you about my dad. He passed away this morning, but before he did so, he said that yesterday was the happiest day of his entire life." As I heard that message, I thanked God for the inspiration that came to me in the twinkling of an eye to invite this good man to come forward and receive the plaudits of his stake members, whom he had served, while he was yet alive and able to enjoy them. I thank my Heavenly Father for his wife, for his family, and for the service they continue to render so beautifully to their fellowmen.

As we love our God, as we love our neighbor, we can be the recipients of our Heavenly Father's love. Of all the blessings I have had in my life, one of the sweetest is that feeling the Lord provides when I know that He has answered the prayer of another person through me. As we love the Lord, as we love our neighbor, we discover that our Heavenly Father will answer the prayers of others through our ministry.

This chapter is adapted from a fourteen-stake
address delivered at Brigham Young University
October 11, 1981.

15

You Make a Difference

Davids declares in one of his beautiful and moving psalms, "O Lord our Lord, how excellent is thy name in all the earth! . . . When I consider thy heavens, the work of thy fingers, the moon and the stars, which thou hast ordained; what is man, that thou art mindful of him?" (Psalm 8:1, 3-4.)

Job, that righteous man of old, joined in the question when he asked, "What is man, that thou shouldest magnify him? and that thou shouldest set thine heart upon him?" (Job 7:17.)

A person need not grope for answers to these penetrating questions when he knows that he is part of "a chosen generation, a royal priesthood, an holy nation," "a spiritual house, an holy priesthood." (1 Peter 2:9, 5.)

As bearers of the priesthood, we have been placed on earth in troubled times. We live in a complex world with currents of conflict everywhere to be found. Political machinations ruin the stability of nations, despots grasp for power, and segments of society seem forever downtrodden, deprived of opportunity, and left with feelings of failure.

We who have been ordained to the priesthood of God can make a difference. When we qualify for the help of the

Lord, we can build boys, we can mend men, we can accomplish miracles in His holy service. Our opportunities are without limit.

Though the task looms large, we are strengthened by the truth: "The greatest force in this world today is the power of God as it works through man." If we are on the Lord's errand, we are entitled to the Lord's help. That divine help, however, is predicated upon our worthiness. To sail safely the seas of mortality, to perform a human rescue mission, we need the guidance of that eternal mariner — even the great Jehovah. We reach out, we reach up, to obtain heavenly help.

Are our reaching hands clean? Are our yearning hearts pure? Looking backward in time through the pages of history, a lesson on worthiness is gleaned from the words of the dying King Darius. Darius, through the proper rites, had been recognized as legitimate king of Egypt. His rival, Alexander the Great, had been declared legitimate son of Ammon. He, too, was Pharaoh. Alexander, finding the defeated Darius on the point of death, laid his hands upon his head to heal him, commanded him to arise and resume his kingly power, and concluded, "I swear unto thee, Darius, by all the gods, that I do these things truly and without fakery." Darius replied with a gentle rebuke, "Alexander, my boy, . . . do you think you can touch heaven with those hands of yours?" (From a paper by Hugh Nibley, "No Idle Tale: Some Egyptian Elements in the Book of Abraham.")

An inspiring lesson is learned from a "Viewpoint" article that appeared recently in the Church News section of the *Deseret News*. May I quote:

"To some it may seem strange to see ships of many nations loading and unloading cargo along the docks at Portland, Oregon. That city is 100 miles from the ocean. Getting there involves a difficult, often turbulent passage over the bar guarding the Columbia River and a long trip up the Columbia and Willamette Rivers.

"But ship captains like to tie up at Portland. They know that as their ships travel the seas, a curious saltwater shellfish called a barnacle fastens itself to the hull and stays there for the rest of its life, surrounding itself with a rock-like shell. As more and more barnacles attach themselves, they increase the ship's drag, slow its progress, decrease its efficiency.

"Periodically, the ship must go into dry dock, where with great effort the barnacles are chiseled or scraped off. It's a difficult, expensive process that ties up the ship for days. But not if the captain can get his ship to Portland. Barnacles can't live in fresh water. There, in the sweet, fresh waters of the Willamette or Columbia, the barnacles loosen and fall away, and the ship returns to its task lightened and renewed.

"Sins are like those barnacles. Hardly anyone goes through life without picking up some. They increase the drag, slow our progress, decrease our efficiency. Unrepented, building up one on another, they can eventually sink us.

"In His infinite love and mercy, our Lord has provided a harbor where, through repentance, our barnacles fall away and are forgotten. With our souls lightened and renewed, we can go efficiently about our work and His."

A loving Heavenly Father has provided, for our guidance, models to follow, individuals who have made a difference in their own times. I choose to call these noble souls pioneers. Webster defines a pioneer as "one who goes before, showing others the way to follow." With faith as their moving power, they sailed upstream against the currents of doubt that surrounded them. We cannot help but be inspired in our efforts as we remember their examples.

117

From Nephi: "I will go and do the things which the Lord hath commanded." (1 Nephi 3:7.)

From Samuel: "To obey is better than sacrifice, and to hearken than the fat of rams." (1 Samuel 15:22.)

From Paul: "I am not ashamed of the gospel of Christ: for it is the power of God unto salvation." (Romans 1:16.)

From Job: "I know that my redeemer liveth." (Job 19:25.)

From Joseph Smith: "I am calm as a summer's morning, for I have a conscience void of offense towards God, and towards all men." (D&C 135:4.)

These noble leaders made a difference in their own times. What about today? How about you and me?

The world felt the quickening pace of activity when President Spencer W. Kimball declared, "We must lengthen our stride." He stepped forward and the Church followed.

When President Ezra Taft Benson warned that we had neglected the Book of Mormon and urged every member to read and study this sacred volume, new printing presses were required to produce more and more copies of the book, as boys and girls and men and women followed the prophet in his own reading and in his inspired declaration. Every day letters arrive at the president's office that testify to the enrichment of lives that comes from reading the Book of Mormon. They tell of families united, goals attained, and souls saved. Such is the power of a prophet.

We do not have a monopoly on goodness. There are God-fearing men and women in all nations who influence for good those with whom they associate. I think of the founder of Scouting, Lord Baden-Powell, and those who teach and live the principles he advocated. Who can measure the far-reaching effect on human lives of the Scout Oath:

"On my honor I will do my best to do my duty to God

and my country and to obey the Scout Law; to help other people at all times; to keep myself physically strong, mentally awake and morally straight."

Impossible of calculation is the result for good when men and boys observe the Scout Law: trustworthy, loyal, helpful, friendly, courteous, kind, obedient, cheerful, thrifty, brave, clean, and reverent.

The influence of personal testimonies is ever so far reaching. The Lord instructed: "The testimony which ye have borne is recorded in heaven for the angels to look upon; and they rejoice over you, and your sins are forgiven you." (D&C 62:3.)

He also cautioned us: "With some I am not well pleased, for they will not open their mouths, but they hide the talent which I have given unto them, because of the fear of man." (D&C 60:2.)

We never know when our turn will come to comply with the admonition of Peter to "be ready always to give an answer to every man that asketh you a reason of the hope that is in you." (1 Peter 3:15.)

Some years ago I had an opportunity to address a business convention in Dallas, Texas, sometimes called "the city of churches." After the convention, I took a sightseeing bus tour about the city's suburbs. Our driver would comment, "On the left you see the Methodist Church," or "There on the right is the Catholic cathedral."

As we passed a beautiful red brick building situated upon a hill, the driver explained, "That building is where the Mormons meet." A woman in the rear of the bus asked, "Driver, can you tell us something about the Mormons?" The driver steered the bus to the side of the road, turned about in his seat, and replied, "Lady, all I know about the Mormons is that they meet in that red brick building. Is there anyone on this bus who knows anything about the Mormons?"

I gazed at the expression on each person's face for some sign of recognition, some desire to comment. I found nothing—not a sign. Then I realized the truth of the statement, "When the time for decision arrives, the time for preparation is past." For the next fifteen minutes I had the privilege of sharing with others my testimony concerning The Church of Jesus Christ of Latter-day Saints.

The seeds of testimony frequently do not take root and flower immediately. Bread cast upon the water returns, at times only after many days.

I answered the ring of my telephone one evening to hear a voice ask, "Are you related to an Elder Monson who years ago served in the New England Mission?" I answered that such was not the case. The caller introduced himself as a Brother Leonardo Gambardella and then mentioned that an Elder Monson and an Elder Bonner had called at his home long ago and had borne their personal testimonies to him. He had listened but had done nothing further to apply their teachings. Subsequently he moved to California, where, after some thirteen years, he again found the truth and was converted and baptized. Brother Gambardella then asked if there were a way he could reach these elders who first had visited with him, so that he might express to them his profound gratitude for their testimonies, which had remained with him.

I checked the records. I located the elders. Can you imagine their surprise when, now married with families of their own, I telephoned them and told them the good news—even the culmination of their early efforts. They remembered Brother Gambardella and, at my suggestion, telephoned him to extend their congratulations and welcome him into the Church.

Each person can make a difference. Whom the Lord calls, the Lord qualifies. This promise extends not only to missionaries, but also to home teachers, quorum leaders, presidents of branches, and bishops of wards. When we qualify ourselves by our worthiness, when we strive with faith, nothing wavering, to fulfill the duties appointed to us, when we seek the inspiration of the Almighty in the performance of our responsibilities, we can achieve the miraculous.

Let us hearken to the hymn, "Improve the Shining Moments":

> Time flies on wings of lightning;
> We cannot call it back.
> It comes, then passes forward
> Along its onward track.
> And if we are not mindful,
> The chance will fade away;
> For life is quick in passing.
> 'Tis as a single day.

Let us determine to shed any barnacles of sin, to prepare for our time of opportunity, and to honor our church membership through the service we render, the lives we bless, and the souls we are privileged to help save.

16

Heavenly Homes, Forever Families

We are frequently reminded by song and the spoken word that "the home is the basis of a righteous life, and no other instrumentality can take its place nor fulfill its essential functions." (The First Presidency, 1962.)

Actually, a home is much more than a house. A house may be constructed of lumber, brick, and stone. A home is made of love, sacrifice, and respect. A house can be a home, and a home can be a heaven when it shelters a family. Like the structure in which it dwells, the family may be large or small. It may be old or young. It may be in excellent condition or it may show signs of wear, of neglect, of deterioration.

Some Latter-day Saint families are comprised of mother, father, sons, and daughters all at home, while others have witnessed the tender departure of one, then another, then another of its members. Occasionally only one member remains. The family, however, continues—for families are forever.

Whether we are preparing to establish our own family or simply considering how to bring heaven closer to our present home, we can learn from the Lord. He is the master architect. He has taught us how we must build.

When Jesus walked the dusty pathways of towns and

villages that we now reverently call the Holy Land and taught His disciples by beautiful Galilee, He often spoke in parables, in language the people understood best. Frequently He referred to home building in relationship to the lives of those who listened.

He declared: "Every . . . house divided against itself shall not stand." (Matthew 12:25.) Later He cautioned: "Behold, mine house is a house of order . . . and not a house of confusion." (D&C 132:8.)

In a revelation given through the Prophet Joseph Smith at Kirtland, Ohio, on December 17, 1832, the Master counseled: "Organize yourselves; prepare every needful thing; and establish a house, even a house of prayer, a house of fasting, a house of faith, a house of learning, a house of glory, a house of order, a house of God." (D&C 88:119.)

Where could any of us locate a more suitable blueprint whereby he could wisely and properly build? Such a house would meet the building code outlined in Matthew, even a house built "upon a rock" (see Matthew 7:24-25), a house capable of withstanding the rains of adversity, the floods of opposition, and the winds of doubt everywhere present in our challenging world.

Some might ask, "But that revelation was to provide guidance for the construction of a temple. Is it relevant today?"

I would respond: "Did not the Apostle Paul declare, 'Know ye not that ye are the temple of God, and that the Spirit of God dwelleth in you?' " (1 Corinthians 3:16.)

Let the Lord be the General Contractor for the family—even the home—we build. Then each of us can be subcontractors responsible for a vital segment of the whole project. All of us are thereby builders. Hence, I speak to all participants and provide guidelines from God, lessons from life, and points to ponder as we commence to build.

Point number one: *Kneel down to pray.*

"Trust in the Lord with all thine heart; and lean not unto thine own understanding. In all thy ways acknowledge him, and he shall direct thy paths." (Proverbs 3:5-6.) So spoke the wise Solomon, the son of David, King of Israel.

On the American continent, Jacob, the brother of Nephi, declared: "Look unto God with firmness of mind, and pray unto him with exceeding faith." (Jacob 3:1.)

This divinely inspired counsel comes to us today as crystal clear water to a parched earth. We live in troubled times. Doctors' offices throughout the land are filled with individuals who are beset with emotional problems as well as physical distress. Our divorce courts are doing a land-office business because people have unsolved problems. Personnel workers and grievance committees in modern industry work long hours in an effort to assist people with their problems.

One personnel officer, assigned to handle petty grievances, concluded an unusually hectic day by placing in jest a small sign on his desk for those with unsolved problems. It read, "Have you tried prayer?" What that personnel officer did not know when he placed such a sign upon his desk was that he was providing counsel and direction that would solve more problems, alleviate more suffering, prevent more transgression, and bring about greater peace and contentment in the human soul than could be obtained in any other way.

A prominent American judge was asked what we, as citizens of the countries of the world, could do to reduce crime and disobedience to law and to bring peace and contentment into our lives and into our nations. He thoughtfully

125

replied, "I would suggest a return to the old-fashioned practice of family prayer."

As a people, aren't we grateful that family prayer is not an out-of-date practice with us? There is not a more beautiful sight in all this world than to see a family praying together. There is real meaning behind the oft-quoted adage: "The family that prays together stays together."

The Lord directed that we have family prayer when He said: "Pray in your families unto the Father, always in my name, that your wives and your children may be blessed." (3 Nephi 18:21.)

Will you join me as we look in on a typical Latter-day Saint family offering prayers unto the Lord? Father, mother, and each of the children kneel, bow their heads, and close their eyes. A sweet spirit of love, unity, and peace fills the home. As father hears his tiny son pray unto God that his dad will do the right things and be obedient to the Lord's bidding, do you think that such a father would find it difficult to honor the prayer of his precious son? As a teenage daughter hears her sweet mother plead unto God that her daughter will be inspired in the selection of her companions, that she will prepare herself for a temple marriage, don't you believe that such a daughter will seek to honor this humble, pleading petition of her mother whom she so dearly loves? When father, mother, and each of the children earnestly pray that the fine sons in the family will live worthy, that they may in due time receive a call to serve as ambassadors of the Lord in the mission fields of the Church, don't we begin to see how such sons grow to young manhood with an overwhelming desire to serve as missionaries?

As we offer unto God our family prayers and our personal prayers, let us do so with faith and trust in Him. If we have been slow to hearken to the counsel to pray always, there is no finer hour to begin than now. Those who feel that prayer might denote a physical weakness should remember that individuals never stand taller than when they are upon their knees.

Point number two: *Step up to serve.*

For our example, we turn to the life of the Lord. Like a glowing searchlight of goodness is the life of Jesus as He ministered among men. He brought strength to the limbs of the cripple, sight to the eyes of the blind, hearing to the ears of the deaf, and life to the body of the dead.

His parables preach power. With the good Samaritan, He taught: "Love thy neighbour." Through His kindness to the woman taken in adultery, He taught compassionate understanding. In His parable of the talents, He taught us to improve ourselves and to strive for perfection. Well could He have been preparing us for our building role in the eternal family. Those who are lifting are not leaning. Those who are serving are not sulking.

An example of stepping up to serve is found in the life of our prophet, President Ezra Taft Benson, and the family of which he is a member. President Benson has described to the General Authorities how his father was called to fill a mission. He left behind his wife, who was expecting another child, his seven children, his farm, and all that he had. Did he lose anything? President Benson tells how his mother would gather the family around the kitchen table and there, by the flickering light of an oil-fueled lamp, read the letters from her husband. Several times during the reading there would be a pause to wipe away the tears that flowed freely. The result? Each of the children later served a mission. Each stepped up to serve.

Point number three: *Reach out to rescue.*

On the journey along the pathway of life, there are casualties. Some depart from the road markers that lead to life eternal, only to discover that the detour chosen ultimately leads to a dead end. Indifference, carelessness, selfishness, and sin all take their costly toll in human lives. There are those who, for unexplained reasons, march to the sound of a different drummer, later to learn they have followed the Pied Piper of sorrow and suffering.

As the year 1985 drew to its end, the First Presidency took note of those who had strayed from the fold of Christ and issued a special statement entitled "An Invitation to Come Back." The message contained this appeal: "We encourage Church members to forgive those who may have wronged them. To those who have ceased activity and to those who have become critical, we say, 'Come back. Come back and feast at the table of the Lord and taste again the sweet and satisfying fruits of fellowship with the saints.' We are confident that many have longed to return but have felt awkward about doing so. We assure you that you will find open arms to receive you and willing hands to assist you."

Perhaps an oft-repeated scene will bring closer to home your personal opportunity to reach out to rescue. Let us look in on a family with a lad named Jack. Throughout Jack's early life, he and his father had many serious arguments. One day, when Jack was seventeen, they had a particularly violent quarrel. Jack said to his father, "This is the straw that breaks the camel's back. I'm leaving home, and I will never return!" So declaring, he went to his room and packed a bag. His mother begged him to stay, but he was too angry to listen. He left her crying at the doorway.

Leaving the yard, Jack was about to pass through the

gate when he heard his father call to him: "Jack, I know that a large share of the blame for your leaving rests with me. For this I am truly sorry. I want you to know that if you should ever wish to return home, you'll always be welcome. And I'll try to be a better father to you. I want you to know that I'll always love you." Jack said nothing, but went to the bus station and bought a ticket to a distant point. As he sat in the bus watching the miles go by, he thought about the words of his father. He realized how much love it had required for his father to do what he had done. Dad had apologized. He had invited him back and had left the words ringing in the summer air, "I love you."

It was then that Jack understood that the next move was up to him. He knew that the only way he could ever find peace with himself was to demonstrate to his father the same kind of maturity, goodness, and love that Dad had shown toward him. Jack got off the bus, bought a return ticket to home, and went back.

He arrived shortly after midnight, entered the house, and turned on the light. There in the rocking chair sat his father, his head bowed. As the father looked up and saw Jack, he rose from the chair, and they rushed into each other's arms. Jack often said, "Those last years that I was home were among the happiest of my life."

Here was a boy who overnight became a man. Here was a father who, suppressing passion and bridling pride, reached out to rescue his son before he became one of that vast "lost battalion" resulting from fractured families and shattered homes. Love was the binding band, the healing balm. Love — so often felt, so seldom expressed.

From Mount Sinai there thunders in our ears: "Honour thy father and thy mother." (Exodus 20:12.) And later, from

129

that same God, the injunction: "Live together in love." (D&C 42:45.)

Kneel down to pray. Step up to serve. Reach out to rescue. Each is a vital page of God's blueprint to make a house a home and a home a heaven.

Let us build with skill, take no shortcuts, and follow His blueprint. Then the Lord, even our building inspector, may say to us, as He said when He appeared to Solomon, a builder of another day, "I have hallowed this house, which thou hast built, to put my name there for ever; and mine eyes and mine heart shall be there perpetually." (1 Kings 9:3.) We will then have heavenly homes and forever families.

INDEX

N

Neighbor, love of, 110-11
New Testament, 58
Nibley, Hugh, 116
Nickerson, Freeman, 13
Nielsen, Peter, 16

O

Obedience to law, 86-88

P

Page, John E., 105-6
Patriarch: definition of, 37; humility of, 38
Patriarchal blessing: as a Liahona, 36, 39, 40; as a revelation, 38; personal nature of, 38-39
Perfection: examples of, 5; guideposts to, 86
Petersen, Mark E., 102
Prayer: as a guide to life, 6; in Scouting, 24; power of personal, 101; family, 125-27
Pratt, Parley P., 14
Premortal life, 2-3
Priesthood bearers: can make a difference, 115, 121; opportunities for, 115-16; power of, 116; examples of, 118
Primary president, 77-78
Prophet, power of, 118

R

Race of life, 5-6
Reading, pleasure of, 100

Rescue, reach out to, 128-29
Respect for others, 88-90
Resurrection, testimonies of, 7-8
Richards, Stephen L, 5
Rigdon, Sidney, 13-14
Rooker, Clifton, 113-14
Rosetti, Christina Georgina, poem by, 50

S

Sandburg, Carl, quotation from, 85-86
Scouting: builds boys, 19; education in, 21-22; love in, 22-23; service in, 23-25; oath, 118-19; law, 118-19
Scriptures: as a guide, 6; examples of courage from, 66-67
Seattle Temple, 79
Self-mastery, 90-92
Service: in Scouting, 23-25; anonymous, 29-31; begins with individual, 74-75; joy in, 92-93; indicates love for God, 105-6, 108, 114; in Church assignments, 111; stepping up to, 127
Sin, shunning, 98-99
Smith, George Albert, 46-47
Smith, Jan, 76
Smith, Joseph: testimony of, 8; as a missionary, 13-14; courage of, 67; on happiness, 74; on preparing temples, 80, 124; calls missionary, 105-6
Smith, Joseph Fielding, 65
Smith, Samuel, 13

Index

Soul, worth of, 11-2
Spencer, Catherine Curtis, 108
Spencer, Orson, 108
Spender, Stephen, quotation
by, 29
St. George Tabernacle, 15-16
Stake presidency, call to, 65
Stein, Joseph, 97
Stuart, J. E. B., quotation from,
66

T

Tabernacle, story of windows
for the, 15-16
Tale of Two Cities, 86
Temple: Seattle, 79; teachings
of, 80; Idaho Falls, 95
Ten Commandments, 87
Tennyson, Alfred, Lord, 46
Testimony, sharing, 103-4,
119-20
Teton Dam disaster, 92-93
Truth, living the, 99-103

V

Vanderbilt, Alfred, 29
Van Dyke, Henry, story by,
31-33

W

Welch, Charlie, 24-25
Widows: definition of, 41;
Christ's concern for, 42;
author visits, 44-46; Church
leaders concerned about, 47;
boys visit, 52-53
Winters, E. Francis, 61
Woodruff, Robert W., quotation from, 21
Wordsworth, William, poem
by, 2-3

Y

Young, Phineas, 13

135